ONE LAST DANCE WITH THE DANI TRIBE

HARLAN FLICK

Lovstad Publishing
Madison, Wisconsin/Yuma, Arizona
Lovstadpublishing@gmail.com

ONE LAST DANCE WITH THE DANI TRIBE
First Edition

ISBN: 1977740316
ISBN-13: 978-1977740311

Printed in the United States of America

Cover design by Lovstad Publishing
All photographs are the property of the author.

This book is dedicated to Wali, Chief of Opaghima Village
and Killian, Chief of Wiyagoba Village.

It is also dedicated to all of the Dani villagers
who shared with us the generosity of their time,
their culture, and their friendship.

CONTENTS

ONE LAST DANCE WITH THE DANI TRIBE

<h1 align="center">1</h1>

A SHORT HISTORY OF NEW GUINEA

The history of New Guinea is long, complex, and often bloody. New Guinea has been controlled by multiple countries, occupied by the Japanese during World War II, and, one could argue, the western portion of the island had its independence stolen by the Indonesian government.

New Guinea is the second largest island in the world encompassing approximately one percent of the world's land mass. Only Greenland has a larger land mass than New Guinea. New Guinea lies in the Southwest Pacific region.

It remains a land of jungles, swamps, majestic peaks as high as 10,000 feet, and mountain valleys. It is home to fifteen foot salt water crocodiles, wild pigs, the smallest parrots in the world and the gigantic cassowary birds. There are a whole variety of fish, some of which are found nowhere else on earth. It was also home to headhunters, cannibals, and warring tribes. It has had a history of colonization, conquest, and control by foreign nations. Much of its history over who controls the island has been bathed in blood. New Guinea has been controlled by multiple countries, occupied by the Japanese during World War II, and, one could argue, the western portion of the island had its independence stolen by the Indonesian government.

The Spanish and the Portuguese were the first Europeans to set foot on New Guinea soil. The Portuguese may have been the first Europeans to arrive in the 1520's. Both countries had explored the Spice Islands for their lucrative spice trade and eventually this lead to the discovery of New Guinea.

The land, originally called Papua, was later renamed New Guinea because, it was thought, the indigenous people resembled the natives of Guinea, Africa, with the short, brown, frizzled quality of their hair.

The Dutch later gained control of the island and began colonizing and establishing outposts along coastal areas. The Dutch laid claim to the island as part of the Netherlands East Indies. They renamed the island Nieuw Guinea.

The Dutch also claimed control of Indonesia in 1800. They wanted to gain total control of the spice trade and the lucrative cash crops that could be exported back to Europe. The name "Irian" was used in the Indonesian language to refer to the island, and the Indonesian province as Irian Jaya Province. Irian Jaya means "To Rise" or "Rising Spirit."

The British, not to be outdone by the Dutch, claimed the eastern part of the island as a British Protectorate. They renamed this eastern part of New Guinea in 1888; they called it British New Guinea.

In 1902, the British placed the authority of British New Guinea in the hands of the Commonwealth of Australia. The name was changed once again to the Territory of Papua. Papua finally became an independent country in 1975 as the country of Papua New Guinea.

New Guinea was invaded by the Japanese in 1942. It would become a key battleground in the Southwest Pacific Theater throughout World War II.

The natives, Papuans, gave assistance to the Allies throughout the war. Approximately 216,000 Japanese, Australian, and U.S. sailors, soldiers, and airmen lost their lives while fighting in the jungles of New Guinea. Many native Papuans also lost their lives while aiding the Allies, but no official account of their deaths was ever recorded.

Indonesia retained control of western New Guinea after World War II. Many western Papuans wanted their own independence and conflicts arose between the Indonesian government and those living in Western New Guinea. Finally, in 1969 under the "Act of Free Choice," all men and women of Western New Guinea were to go to the polls to vote whether to become an independent country or to remain a part of Indonesia.

Under President Suharto, a general was sent to Western New Guinea to oversee the voting. With a strong military presence in place, this general chose 1,050 hand-picked men and women to vote on independence. The chosen men and women were coerced, by threat of death to them and their families, to vote in favor of remaining a part of Indonesia. When asked how they would vote, all 1,050 men and women raised their hands voting for Western New Guinea to remain a part of Indonesia. In Western New Guinea, this vote became known as, "The Act of No Choice."

Over forty years later there remains an independence

faction in Western New Guinea. There was a demonstration in 2011 which was quickly put down by Indonesian forces. Since 1963, many Papuans have been under surveillance, many of whom have been tortured or killed by Indonesian police.

Australia supported the elections and the United Nations rubber stamped the Act of Free Choice.

Even though it was a sham election, Western New Guinea remains a part of Indonesia to this day.

There remains a large population of Papuans living in Australia. The latest in a long line of activists is the West Papuan Freedom Flotilla who still holds demonstrations for the right of Western New Guinea to gain independence from Indonesia.

Western New Guinea today is called Papua. The Eastern portion of the island is the independent nation of Papua, New Guinea.

When we traveled into the interior of Western New Guinea in 1980, the provincial capital was still Jayapura and the area where the Dani tribes lived, was still called Irian Jaya. Please keep those thoughts in mind as you travel with us into the land of the Dani tribes.

2
GETTING FROM WISCONSIN TO JAKARTA, INDONESIA

The year was 1978; my wife, Pam, and I were just starting our first year of teaching at Jakarta International School in Jakarta, Indonesia. Pam was a business education teacher while I held down a position in the Physical Education Department.

We had come to Jakarta on the shirt tails of a friend who had discovered the opportunities that teaching at international schools presented. My friend and I kept in contact over a three year period by making voice tapes and sending them back and forth between Wisconsin and Indonesia. My friend kept extolling the virtues of this international school and the lifestyle that living in Indonesia promised. It would take those three years, and many cassettes crossing between Indonesia and Wisconsin, to convince us to accept a brokered invitation to interview with the Superintendent of Jakarta International School. Believe me when I say that both my wife and I had been bred and born in Wisconsin, and we had every intention of staying and growing old in our home state. More voice tapes crossed oceans, my wife and I had both switched schools once already and our opinions of teaching outside the friendly confines of continental United States began to sprout and send up tiny chutes of interest.

We finally agreed to an interview to take place at the Chicago O'Hare Hilton in late February. International schools recruit earlier than stateside schools because of the time needed to secure visas, work permits, medical exams and inoculations, as well as other related legal documents required to work in a foreign country.

My friend said he had already spoken to the superintendent about us, so we felt a bit conflicted about turning down an interview and disappointing this friend after he had gone through the trouble of putting in a good word on our behalf. We quickly put the interview out of our minds and went back to teaching our classes.

February dawned, cold and snowy, inching along at a snail's pace, as Wisconsin winters have a tendency to do. The days were bleak and overcast, with cold nights, going and coming home from school in the dark was the norm. We were Midwest folks; we come from hearty stock and we were used to the vagaries of winters in the Midwest.

The date finally arrived for the interview and we both wondered why we had ever agreed to the interview in the first place. Being Midwesterners, in other words people used to keeping their word, we loaded into our car for the trip to Chicago. Unfortunately a heavy, early evening snowstorm arrived just as we were about to leave Madison. Snow piled up with each passing mile, the wind picked up and intelligent drivers got off the highways as they saw cars sliding off the road. We drove blindly on, snow swirling around us, trying to locate the O'Hare International Airport and the O'Hare Hilton.

Remember this is long before the arrival of GPS technology in cars that help us find locations so easily today.

Just about the time we were ready to give up, turn around, and return to Madison, forgetting any thought of teaching abroad, we saw the blinking lights of the airport through the falling snow.

The O'Hare Hilton was easy enough to find once we located the airport turnoff and in a few minutes we had parked the car, entered the hotel and were soon in the room of Denzel Widel, Ph.D., Superintendent of Jakarta International School.

The interview went well. We were convinced we would not be offered contracts at this prestigious school, so we relaxed and enjoyed the experience. Den Widel had a friendly, engaging personality and the interview was more of a conversation than an interview. It wasn't like any interview we had ever experienced previously so we thought he probably wasn't that interested in us as candidates.

After we had talked for an extended period of time, Dr. Widel produced a photo album that would ultimately change our lives. He mentioned that the school was located on two separate campuses and that we would be teaching on the larger, 22 acre campus. As we looked at each photo, the possibility of a whole new world opened up before us. The campus was extraordinarily beautiful. Round, modular classrooms dotted the campus, with lush green spaces between each building. Flowering shrubs, frangipani trees, palm trees, and open court yards with students milling about reminded us both of a college campus. It was hard to compare what we were seeing in the photos with the stand alone public school buildings we were used to in Wisconsin. The students, we were told, when not in class could congregate around the campus grounds, free to go to an open air cafeteria, or small kiosks, set up around a courtyard area where they could purchase snacks and drinks.

The one photo in the album that changed our minds, and ultimately our lives, was a photo of Andy Norman, the high school music teacher. He was giving a lunch time concert with some of his music students. The concert was being held under palm and frangipani trees on campus. We noticed the photo and looked at the gathering of students enjoying the mid-day concert under sparkling blue skies.

We had just driven down to Chicago in a blinding snowstorm and I don't think either my wife or I could get that photo out of our minds as we drove back to Madison in frigid temperatures with snow swirling around us, a white apparition, beckoning for change.

We had to wait three weeks before we received a telephone call offering us positions at the school. We had taken a week to mull over a move of this magnitude. We had no children, had only been married a year, and like most newlyweds, had few possessions. We were young, and more than a bit naive. We felt we could live almost any place in the world for a short period of time. The initial contract was for two years. We would have preferred a one year contract, but after a very short discussion we signed the contracts, confident that two years would be the extent of our overseas experiment in international education. After two years, we knew we would be more than ready to return to Wisconsin and our Midwestern roots. We felt confident that we could get another teaching job in public education and finish our teaching and coaching careers back in Wisconsin. The good old U.S.A. would surely call us back to hearth and home. All we had to do was survive for two years. During that time, we knew we'd have so many opportunities to travel that the time would pass quickly.

We turned in our letters of resignation effective at the end of that current school year and told a few teaching friends we were off to Southeast Asia in August of 1978. Our colleagues were overwhelmingly supportive once we told them what the school was like and the financial package the school was offering. A common refrain from our friends went something like this: "Wow, what an adventure. You are so lucky you are young and don't have any kids. We'd do it in a minute, but we can't uproot our children."

Other comments were, "If we didn't have the mortgage on the house hanging over our heads, we'd jump at the chance to teach at a school like that." Another common refrain was, "We'd love this opportunity, but my parents (or my wife's parents) would freak out if we left the states. They really couldn't handle it. They would constantly be worried about our safety."

Once we arrived in Jakarta we found teachers with mortgages back in their home country, others had children they'd uprooted, and still others had parents who did worry about their children's safety living in an underdeveloped, third-world country. Our own parents were definitely in that boat.

Neither my wife nor I considered ourselves to be risk takers. We were pretty much vanilla Midwesterners, growing up in tiny rural towns that are ubiquitous throughout Wisconsin. We would learn later that international schools love recruiting Midwesterners for their personal qualities of hard work, showing up on time, being dependable, and working until the job is done. Administrators often told us they like recruiting in the Midwest because, "Midwesterners have a very strong work ethic."

Summer went by quickly and we packed the basic necessities into four suitcases. We received money from the school to more than cover our airfares, gave hugs to our families and friends, and prepared to leave. I was 28 years old and I had never flown on a plane before. Now I was going to fly half way around the world.

We flew out from O'Hare International Airport and landed in Washington D.C. to see my older brother who worked for the government. We spent a few days with him seeing the sights of the D.C. area. We went to the Smithsonian, saw the White House and a few other attractions and then boarded a flight to London. Coming down over London, seeing strange houses with strange roofs and postage stamp lawns confirmed to me that I was no longer in middle America. There were black taxi cabs that looked like they came out of the 1930's, strange British accents, overcast skies that seemed to implore rain at any second. There was strange food that seemed quite bland even by our fairly bland Midwestern standards. There were pubs rather than bars, and a restaurant chain called Blimpy's was as close as it came to fast food.

We were only going to stay in London for a few days so we wanted to make the most of it.

We spent the first few days in a jet lag induced fog.

We went to our first professional play, "A Chorus Line," and were amazed by the quality of the actors. We made a side trip out to Stonehenge wondering about the significance of the circular arrangement of stone megaliths of the Neolithic period. We walked around Piccadilly Circus. At Speaker's Corner in Hyde Park, we found that anyone can get up and talk about pretty much any subject they choose. We saw Big Ben and the Tower of London; we remembered a time when the sun never set on the British Empire. Before we knew it, our time had passed, so we said goodbye to England before boarding a plane that would take us to Singapore. Once we landed in Singapore we would have a four day stay in which we would have our visa work and work permits processed.

We were met at the airport by school personnel and escorted to our hotel. We had a four day whirlwind stay in our first Asian city while we were being poked and prodded. We completed finger printing, attended orientation sessions on the school, and tried once again to catch up on sleep. Singapore is at least a 12 hour time change from our home in Wisconsin, so jet-lag was really having an effect on our sleep.

We did have some free time. We wandered the city, saw our first rickshaw drivers, our first cobra snake charmer, and felt the intense equatorial sun sap us of our strength. Singaporeans are a hodgepodge of cultures derived from their Malay, Indian, Chinese, and Eurasian ancestry. I heard dialects I had never heard before. None of it made a bit of sense to me, but by god, the country worked like nothing I had ever experienced.

The Wisconsin friends who had helped arrange the interview, were also in Singapore to help us figure out what we needed to buy for our new life in Jakarta. They encouraged us to visit our first tailor where I had two shirts and shorts made and Pam had a couple of blouses designed.

While I was doing my errands, Pam went out and bought a Noritake dish set, flatware, and other assortments of pots and pans. None of these essential goods, we had been told, would be available in Jakarta. At that time, you couldn't buy a watch, a clock, get a pizza, ice cream or donut in Jakarta, so whatever we wanted, we needed to buy in Singapore and take in suitcases to Jakarta.

Singapore was a clean, beautiful city-state that was beginning to transport itself to a modern city under the leadership of Premier Lee Kwan Yew who took over in 1959 and would become the longest running prime minister in the history of any country.

All taxis had signs reminding them to be friendly and courteous to riders, all part of Mr. Lee's design to turn Singapore into a world class city. Singapore seemed to have rules for everything and Mr. Lee, as he was affectionately called by Singaporeans, ruled with an iron fist. Spitting was not allowed and dirty cars were forbidden. The car owner would be fined until his car was washed and polished to a fine sheen. There were no paper wrappers on the ground and all offences were discouraged by stiff fines. Even leaves were quickly swept up by street workers with little thatched brooms and pans.

If you were waiting for a taxi, you were required to stand in a line like everyone else and woe to the man who decided to jump the queue and bump a passenger ahead of him. Every other person in line would admonish the interloper in the most caustic language until he got back in his proper place in line.

All Singaporeans were expected to work. They worked long hours, often 12 to 15 hours per day, weekends included, and they were also expected to save, save, save. They saved for the future so their life could be better, and the lives of their children could be even more prosperous.

There were canings for those who broke significant rules and civil disobedience was not tolerated. There were no public demonstrations allowed and reporters were thrown in jail for libel if they wrote anything too critical of the government.

Singapore had almost no natural resources, a very small army that could offer little protection if attacked by a larger country, and a population of around five million people. In order to prosper, Mr. Lee turned Singapore into a seaport destination for shipping, and a business hub for foreign corporations. Prime Minister Lee was turning Singapore into a significant City State through discipline, cleanliness, business opportunities, and his own iron will.

Singaporeans, it seemed, were buying what he was selling. There were beautiful botanical gardens, flowering plants, bougainvillea, flame trees, and orchids everywhere. Streets were impeccably clean, traffic moved in unison, and there was a buzz of human activity everywhere. We weren't sure exactly what we were witnessing; we just knew we were witnessing something significant. It would take years before we would fully realize the transformation that is Singapore today, all due to the unwavering leadership of Prime Minister Lee Kwan Yew.

We were told not to expect anything like this in Jakarta, a mere one hour and thirty minute flight away.

We flew out of Singapore to Jakarta after our four day hiatus in a country governed by rules, regulations, courtesy, and cleanliness.

Then, we landed in Jakarta.

3

ADJUSTING TO LIFE IN A THIRD WORLD COUNTRY

It would be an understatement to say that our arrival in Jakarta was a culture shock to all of our sensory systems: sight, sound, taste, and smell. We touched down at Halim Airport, coming in low over rice paddies where farmers were tending their cash crop. The water in the irrigation ditches was a muddy brown, while the rice shoots being pushed into the fertile soil were a brilliant green. The farmers were calf deep in mud, stooped over in conical hats methodically pushing plant chutes into the mud.

We taxied down the runway and disembarked in front of a bare bones arrival terminal. We waited in several lines to pass through the immigration desks and eventually found our way to the conveyor belts to retrieve our luggage.

As we came into the area where the luggage would enter the arrival terminal we found ourselves merging into a melting pot of humanity. Unlike Singaporeans, Indonesians had no concept of a line. In fact, Jakarta was the direct opposite of Singapore. Collecting our bags became a free for all, every man and woman for themselves. There was pushing and shoving by local Indonesians as they reached around us.   Brown hands grabbed at bags as the baggage carousel started spitting out its cargo.

We were not prepared for this, but once again the school had personnel on hand to help navigate the chaos. We were told to keep our elbows extended out from our bodies or expect that locals would move around us to grab their parcels. This seemed like such a rude thing to do, especially arriving from Singapore where bedlam like this would never be tolerated.

Bags were loaded onto carts that had wheels that would wobble or lock up. Many would not steer straight. Sweet smelling clove cigarettes, called Kretek, were being smoked by everyone. Those cigarettes produced a thick smoke ring that hung over the entire terminal.

It was hot and humid; there was no air conditioning, not a fan to be seen except for the hand held variety. Those were being wind milled by a few of the local ladies as they waited for a porter to retrieve their bags from the conveyor belt. We were perspiring, our shirts ringed with sweat marks. It didn't take us long to come to the conclusion that we were in a completely different environment than anything we had ever experienced before. This was chaos. There seemed to be no rules. This was nothing like America, and certainly nothing like Singapore.

Like the true gentleman he was, Denzel Widel was there to greet us. He had brought along his wife, Dorothy, who turned out to be a carbon copy of her husband. She was warm, friendly, and did not have a pretentious bone in her body.

It took an interminable amount of time for the convey belts

to start turning, and even then the luggage came in dribs and drabs. The conveyor belts would drop off a few bags and then stop. You then had to wait an indeterminate amount of time before the next sets of luggage would arrive. It became a waiting game, all eyes on the opening of the chute that would deliver our luggage. We were all tired and sweaty as we watched the chute and listened for the sound of the luggage trolleys approach. There seemed to be no rhyme or reason to the time it took to deliver our luggage. Sometimes it was a short interval between trips to the plane and back and other times it seemed to take forever. As we waited, we continued to perspire and our patience began to wane as the minutes slowly ticked by.

We finally made it to customs inspection where you had to declare what you were bringing into the country. Since we were a large group of foreigners we were asked to open our bags while unfamiliar hands fumbled through our luggage looking for contraband. We were finally all waved through customs after a complete inspection of our bags.

We trudged out into the tropical sun, thirteen recruited teaching couples from America, starting a new life in an unfamiliar land. We were hustled out to several Hi-Ace vans, but not before we had to literally fight our way through throngs of porters. The porters were grabbing at our bags in a mad attempt to carry them to our waiting vehicles in exchange for a few Indonesian Rupiah notes.

The sun was beyond hot. No air moved. The fetid smell of rotting vegetation, fuel oil, and garbage assaulted our senses. The smells, strange and unknown to us, made our stomachs queasy. Sensing our discomfort, we were assured by our hosts that we would be out of the airport area soon and it should be an easy forty minute ride to Cilandak. This was the area where the school was located and where our house awaited our arrival.

The sights and sounds of Jakarta were everywhere. Becaks, three wheeled bicycles with a carriage in front were being peddled by spindly men in t-shirts and shorts. The only thing big about these spindly peddlers were their watermelon sized legs. They were peddling shoppers back to their homes laden with goods from open air markets. Many of the drivers smoked the Kretek cigarettes that we had smelled in the airport. Their bulging legs strained against the weight of the bike, the fruit and vegetable purchases of the passengers, and the weight of the passengers themselves. The becak drivers, we would learn, did this same work day after day, pocketing a few thousand rupiah, making a living for their families.

We travelled on through snarled traffic, inching along, each of us glued to a window, taking in the sights and sounds of our new city. All of a sudden, due to jumbled traffic, the van made a quick stop by a garbage dump. The dump was smoldering with lighted fires slowly compressing the sheer size of the debris.

We were stunned to suddenly be surrounded by maybe twenty beggars. We were shocked by the amount of beggars, but also shaken that the group included a number of children dressed in ragged, dirty clothes. This was the first time most of us had ever come in contact with beggars. There were very few street beggars in Wisconsin and certainly none where we had grown up. It was very disconcerting and made us quite uncomfortable.

The beggars were unkempt; their faces smeared with dirt and grime and hair that had not been washed in a long time. They came at us as one, hands out, faces pressed against the windows of our vehicles, sorrowful faces looking for handouts of food or money. We didn't know whether to avoid them or to roll down the window to give them some money. As time went on, we would learn that beggars are a part of the Asian fabric of life. Children would beg to help support their families' modest income.

Because they spent their days scavenging or begging, these young beggars were not able to attend school. Indonesian public schools, at that time, were not free. There was the cost of school uniforms, books, paper, pencils and some other school fees which were out of the reach of low income families who lived day to day on what little money they could earn from scavenging or begging. With no formal education available to these families, the cycle of poverty would continue. This was the first time we faced the reality of extreme poverty, and it was staring us directly in the face.

Our hosts, alert to our discomfort, tried unsuccessfully to put us at ease. They extended words of assurance that we would be out of the area soon and to not look at, or encourage, the beggars in any way. This was a philosophy we came to understand prevailed in third world societies that the beggar population would just get bigger if it was productive for them to beg. However, we'd also learn that it did not mesh with Muslim belief of helping the poor. It was an unnerving few moments before the traffic began to crawl along leaving behind the street urchins who would return to picking through rubbish piles in hope of finding something worth salvaging.

It was August, 1978. We had finally arrived in Cilandak, a small enclave serving wealthier Indonesian and foreign families. We were now in the southern region of the city of Jakarta that was populated by ten million people. No one really knew the actual population of the city with new arrivals and departures daily from bus stations, trains, and cars. New arrivals were looking to carve out a better life for themselves. Each departure was an acceptance of defeat for the leaving who would be returning to their home villages where life was simpler and wages lower.

We drove past the Cilandak campus of Jakarta International School. All we could see was a quick glance at the fence that surrounded the 22 acres that composed the campus grounds.

The Hi-Ace driver only drove a few more minutes and pulled up along a modern looking house with a gate in front. This, we were told, was our house. Housing was only one of the many perks that went along with working at a world class school. The lease on the house was paid for by the school, as were the utilities. There were servants' quarters in the back of the house. We were to have a maid/housekeeper/cook and a Jaga, basically a night watchman who also doubled as a gardener, gate opener, one who carried in the groceries, did the lawn maintenance, and washed the car. The salary of the jaga was also paid for by the school, but it was our responsibility to pay the salary of the cook. The cook's salary was ridiculously cheap, but more expensive than a jaga. Even in the servant class, there was a pecking order as there was in the rest of the Indonesian society. We would pay our cook around $90 a month. We thought this a ridiculously low salary, but were told that if she worked for an Indonesian family she would only be making a third of that amount and would be expected to work seven days a week. Our cook would work six days a week for us and have Sundays off. Her jobs included cooking breakfast and dinner five days a week and all three meals on Saturdays. She was also responsible for doing the laundry. She slept in a small room in the back of the house. The jaga also had a small room and there was a tiny area in the back for them to cook their meals. This area also doubled as a place to hang up our laundry.

Our luggage was quickly delivered by the jaga, who insisted on carrying everything himself. We were introduced to the servants, whose names we quickly forgot, and all of us stood around looking nervous until our entourage left to deliver other new teachers to their new homes.

That first night in our new home was weird. We were very nervous with these strangers (servants) living with us, people we did not know, and whose names we still had not mastered. After touring the house, darkness descended quickly and we went into our bedroom earlier than normal, nervously locking the door, crawled into bed, and tried to sleep. We had an air conditioner for the first time in our lives. It was noisy and thus provided some necessary white noise to aid our sleep. However, we were still jet lagged. Jakarta is only 6 or 7 degrees below the Equator. So the day and night are evenly split to 12 hours each; sunrise was about 6 a.m. and sunset at 6 p.m. We found there to be about a half hour swing throughout the year, meaning sometimes it was 6:30 before dark fell.

It would take us a while to get used to household help. We were used to doing household chores, making meals, doing laundry, shopping, mowing the lawn, and getting our oil changed in our car. With servants, we would no longer have to do those chores, but initially it was hard for us to give up those tasks we had always done ourselves.

The first problem was the communication gap with the language barrier. We did not speak Bahasa Indonesian, the official language of Indonesia. Many of the cooks did speak some English, especially if they had worked previously for expatriate families. Jagas often spoke no English and they might speak an Indonesian dialect that wasn't even Bahasa.

We would speak with the cook in English, gesticulating at times or pantomime what we wanted to communicate. She, in turn, would speak to the jaga and explain his duties for the day. The job of the jaga was to clip the grass, carry in the groceries, wash the car and the floors, trim the shrubs, water the plants, close the gates to the house, carry out the garbage, and at night guard the house for possible intruders.

In truth, we did have some fear of living in a city of several million residents and having unknown locals living in our house. This fear was really magnified and unjustified on our part. We did very quickly come to trust the system and reap the benefits of household help.

I'm sure to most it seems like an ideal life having servants to do all the mundane tasks that most of us would be glad to hand off to someone else. When things were going well servants were a blessing, but sometimes the servants did not get along and we would have to trouble shoot to keep the household running on an even keel. In rare instances, there were corrupt servants who took advantage by stealing or allowing others to steal from expats. Of course, on occasion, a review of expectations would have to be conducted to get jobs done the way we wanted.

We probably went through three or four sets of servants before we found the right combination for our family. That was not at all unusual and a common refrain in the teachers' lounge was, ". . . does anyone know of a good cook that's available?"

The school, ever thoughtful of any and all necessities, had delivered a large wooden trunk. The trunk belonged to the school and would be expected to be returned to the school at a later date. It was a giant care package to get us through the first few weeks until we learned where to shop, buy food and purchase other necessities. In the trunk were dishes, glasses, cutlery, pots and pans, soap, towels, shampoo, toilet paper and wash cloths. The refrigerator had already been filled by the school with enough food to last more than a week.

Den's wife, Dorothy, had even baked us a coffee cake.

Returning faculty members were paired up with us rookies. Their job was to show us different shops and stores where we could purchase the food and staples we would need. The school even gave them money to take us out to eat at a local restaurant. The faculty could not have been more supportive. Having been rookies themselves once, they wanted us to be happy in our new environment. The faculty soon became our family away from home, throwing small dinner parties on weekends and introducing us into the community of expatriates.

In the weeks that followed, we went through a long orientation process, got to know the layout of the campus, had a Hi-Ace Toyota delivered to our house for our use, again compliments of the school, got used to our servants, learned where to shop and where we could buy a case of Coca Cola from a roadside toko. A toko is a tiny open air shop that sells everything from toothpaste, cigarettes, shampoo or any myriad of small items that could be hung, tacked, or tied to the frame of the toko.

When classes started, we found ourselves introduced to children from nearly 50 countries around the world. The children had to pass an English proficiency exam in order to be enrolled at the school. The school also had an extensive three-tiered ESOL program. The students were the children of expatriates who worked at embassies or multi-national corporations doing business in Indonesia. The students were the best and the brightest students we would ever teach, most speaking multiple languages. They were all university bound and very motivated. They would often start a sentence in one language and finish it in another. It was a very humbling experience for those of us who spoke only English.

Even though we had outstanding facilities, even though the kids were terrific, the faculty outstanding, and the facilities world class, for the first few months in Indonesia I was not a happy camper. I made the mistake that we later recognized all too often in other expatriates, comparing everything in

Indonesia to America. Indonesia would always come out on the short end of that comparison.

I would go to work and come home, go to work and come home, day after day, week after week. I loved teaching and I loved the students, but I always found fault with Indonesia and Indonesians. I suffered from "Americanitis." Nothing in Indonesia was as good as it was in America. I had blinders on, and could not see the good, because I was always comparing what Indonesia didn't have to what America did have.

I might have gone on this way and found a quick exit back to America, but my wife finally ordered me out of the house, forced me to walk around the neighborhood, and told me to stop my negativity about our newly adopted country and its people. As it turned out, that is the best advice I ever got.

I probably started with a ten minute walk just around our housing complex. As time passed, the walks became longer and longer. I started to see rubber trees not a ten minute walk from our house that were being tapped, reminding me of the maple trees of Wisconsin and the drip, drip of sap that would eventually turn into maple syrup. I watched construction workers crushing rocks with small hammers so new roads could be built. I saw them heating up barrels of tar over wood fires to tar new roads where only a path had existed before. I saw locals carrying wares in baskets swinging on a stick anchored on their shoulders. I watched construction workers scaling bamboo scaffolding with no safety harness as workers below threw up bricks one at a time as houses sprang up in our neighborhood. I watched farmers pushing rice shoots into flooded fields, their backs bent for hours at a time, conical hats protecting their heads from the equatorial sun.

I would pass a small stream and see little boys fishing with short bamboo poles. I would hold my hands wide, a universal questions asking how large the fish were that they were catching. They would laugh and hold their fingers an inch apart and say, "kecil," which I would learn meant small. They would show me their catch, tiny fish the size of minnows, their young pride showing. They would talk to me in a language I had yet to learn, but with their help, I would pick up a few simple words. I would come to realize the best way to learn a language would be to talk to children who have an economy with vocabulary and are quite pleased to be teachers.

As I took these daily sojourns around our home in Pondok Indah, which means beautiful garden, I began to pick up a few more words of Indonesian. I learned that "baik" meant good, and "tidak bagus" meant bad. "Terima kasih" meant thank you, "selamat pagi" for good morning, and "selamat malam" for good night. I really never became fluent in the language, but I got by.

In short, I started opening my eyes, stopped comparing everything to a developed country like America with its abundance of natural resources, modern highways and skyscrapers. As my eyes began to open, I began to see the real Indonesia and I slowly started falling in love with the country and its people.

Indonesia is an archipelago, a series of some 17,000 islands, about 4,000 of which are inhabited. The width of the western to eastern most islands of Indonesia would reach from Alaska to Florida. Java, the island we were living on, was the most densely populated land mass on Earth. It contained the largest number of Muslims in the world and each morning we would hear the first of five calls to prayer that governed the lives of our Muslim neighbors.

As time passed we would discover Bali, Island of the Gods, the most famous of the Indonesian islands. With its azure waters and white sandy beaches, it was impossible not to fall in love with Bali. We would spend vacations lazing in the sun, snorkeling, getting massages on the beaches that lasted an hour and cost a dollar. We would watch as women from other parts of the world would get their hair plaited just like the actress, Bo Derek. We would drink fruit juices, freshly squeezed, or feast on fresh fish, lobsters, and fried bananas dipped in cinnamon.

A short car ride from Kuta Beach would deposit us in the hill country town of Ubud, a beautiful and cultural, artistic center surrounded by breathtaking rice terraces, cascading streams, and the Agung River. You could take dance lessons to learn Balinese dance, take art lessons in Balinese painting, or just hang out walking the quaint streets, or sipping Balinese coffee in a restaurant overlooking a bubbling stream. The Balinese are Hindu, not Muslim, and their lifestyle was very laid back, very accepting, very relaxing

While in Jakarta, we would join the Jakarta American Club, an Americans only private club, where the food was good, the pool warm, and the service friendly and efficient. The club was surrounded by housing where some U.S. Embassy personnel lived. It was a quiet enclave and a relief from the bustling, noisy streets of the congested city outside the walls of the club. At that time, it was very common for American teachers to be members at the club. On weekends you would see many of your teacher colleagues eating a western breakfast as they lounged around the swimming pool watching as their children splash about. On occasion, a good game of tennis could also be played.

Another perk the school offered was the use of two cabins in the mountains an hours' drive from Jakarta. The cabins slept ten and were leased by the school. You were allotted your dates for the cabins in a draw once school started. The usual allotment was four times a year for each family, but friends often invited you to join them so you could go to the mountains much more often than the four times you were allotted. It was cooler in the mountains and each cabin contained a small pool. It sometimes took a bit of courage to jump into a very chilly pool and swim a few quick laps. Each morning the banana man and the pineapple man came around to sell all the fruit you wanted for just a couple of dollars. The mountains were a relaxing diversion to the hectic, congested streets of Jakarta. It was a place to unwind, take jungle walks, enjoy the cool evenings, and decompress.

These were just some of the benefits we had through the school. Additionally, we would coach teams and fly off to Singapore or Malaysia for weekend sports trips with our student athletes.

We flew home at the end of the first school year and spent the summer gorging on food we could not get in Indonesia. We ate hot dogs and brats, ice cream, potato salad and burgers off the grill. We fished and camped and swatted mosquitoes.

We split time between both sets of parents since we no longer had an apartment. The summer was great and went by quickly, but by summers' end, we were tired of living out of suitcases, imposing on our families' good will. It was relatively easy to say our goodbyes and once again board a plane for the thirty plus hour flight back to Indonesia.

Our second year in Jakarta was much different. We knew the terrain, where to shop for meat and where to get vegetables. We knew where the flower market was located and could fill our home with fresh flowers for a pittance.

We could fly to Singapore for a weekend and go to Jack's Place, a steak house on Killiny Road, for an air flown steak from Australia served on a sizzling platter, or go to "Cold Storage" to stock up on food we could not get in Indonesia. We went up with an empty suitcase and came back with our suitcase bulging.

Life was good and only getting better, as our initial two year contract came to an end.

We did something at the end of this second year we thought we would never do. We signed on for a third year at Jakarta International School. We were convinced this would be our last year in Jakarta and we only had to sign a one year contract, so sign on the dotted line we did. We were making and saving more money than we ever thought possible. The school paid our local Indonesian taxes and we had United States tax exclusions for working outside the confines of the United States. On top of that, we had U.S. Embassy privileges which allowed us the use of the embassy commissary to buy goods we could not get on the local market. With those privileges, we could buy Oscar Meyer wieners and Jones Farms sausages (both good Wisconsin products), wine, jams and jellies, and even a turkey for Thanksgiving.

We did, of course, miss things from stateside. We missed holidays, weddings and funerals, sports, and the changing of the seasons. In Jakarta, I could go to the greyhound races and play tennis on our school courts where ball boys chased down every errant shot and tossed the ball back to you. We had opportunities to travel to exotic places many times throughout the year. We were becoming spoiled, and we were enjoying ourselves too much to return to Wisconsin.

As we started our third year in Jakarta we had travelled to a number of European countries on breaks, as well as travelling extensively in Indonesia. We had gotten over the differences in foods, smells, geographies and customs. We had gotten used to cockroaches and tiny lizards called cicaks that invaded our Pondok Indah house. It was also impossible to keep the tiny ants out of our house. First they would invade the house and then they would invade the sugar bowls. There was an expression about ants in Indonesia. The first year, the saying goes, you remove all ants from your sugar bowls. The second year you don't bother to remove the ants from your sugar. The third year you live in Indonesia, you request ants in your sugar. We were now in our third year in Indonesia and ants were the least of our worries.

What we didn't realize, as we started our third year, is that we were about to be offered the opportunity of a lifetime. We were going to be offered a chance to go back to prehistoric times, with a prehistoric people. We were about to be offered a chance to go into the wilds of New Guinea.

We were about to get an offer we couldn't refuse.

We were about to be offered a chance to visit the Dani tribes of Irian Jaya.

4

DO YOU WANT TO GO ON A GREAT ADVENTURE?

The school year of 1980 began with a rush of new students. The turnover rate at the school was between twenty and thirty percent each year as companies and embassies rotated their employees to other locations around the globe. Children made friends quickly since none of them knew how long their parents would be stationed in Jakarta.

The same was true for teachers. Teachers rotated in and out. Most stayed beyond three years because the school was terrific and the benefits matched the growing reputation of the school. There were always more teachers arriving than leaving because the schools' student population was growing rapidly as more multinational companies started doing business in Indonesia.

By this time my wife and I were old hands. We were now the ones who got matched up with new hires to show them where to shop, how to bargain with shop owners, and where the best restaurants were located.

The first month of school was always very hectic. New students were arriving daily and we had to help them get acclimated to classes, procedures, and the culture of the school. Although the largest percentage of students were American, about forty percent, most were not. The school systems they came from, and were used to, could be quite different than the one they were now entering.

Teachers at the two campuses were well compensated, but along with the terrific compensation package came certain expectations by the school. We were all expected to work extra hours, making sure the school ran like a well oiled machine. We came to school early, stayed after school to work with kids in the many clubs and activities that the school offered, and helped make the transition for students as seamless as possible.

Things were humming along, September had rolled over into October and new students were acclimating to their new environment. We were all too busy to think about when our next vacation would happen or where we might end up travelling.

I can't remember for sure when I first met Gene Wasosky and his wife Kathy, but it didn't take long before we were close friends. Gene worked in the science department and Kathy was an art teacher. The school had softball teams, both men's and women's, that played in a league with other expatriate teams. All of the games were played on our campus because we had a softball field which was the only lighted field in Jakarta, allowing all games to be played in the evenings.

Playing softball was as much a social event as an athletic one. It was a chance to unwind from the daily grind of school, sweat off a pound or two on a warm tropical evening. Most of the team would tip a couple cold ones after the game before heading home to bed. Neither Gene nor I would ever be confused as being a real benefit to the softball team. We were simply role players to our more talented teammates and maybe that is why we became friends.

Gene did, however, have other talents. He was an outstanding squash player and a budding entrepreneur. There were no videos in Jakarta, but Gene found a way to get some videos shipped into the country. Don't ask me how he did this because supposedly you couldn't get videos shipped into Indonesia, but Gene was always one of those guys who knew somebody, who knew somebody. Gene always thought outside the box, and soon he had started a video club. We would show up at his house on Sunday afternoons and watch a selection of videos. For the right to attend this Sunday afternoon ritual, we all paid a small fee to Gene. There seemed to always be some other little side business that Gene would come up with to help enrich his coffers.

He taught himself Bahasa Indonesian, the official language of Indonesia, by reading an Indonesian newspaper, cover to cover, every day. He methodically looked up words that he didn't understand.

Who does stuff like that?

Most of the faculty went to restaurants on the weekends. We were too busy during the week with our jobs, but the weekend was our time to relax, find a decent restaurant and enjoy a good meal. Gene would organize a small group, find some new restaurant that sounded interesting, and we would head out to fight Jakarta traffic and usually locate the restaurant after Gene made a few stops to ask the locals for directions. That, in a nutshell was Gene Wasosky. He was a can do kind of guy, never taking no for an answer, finding a way to get what he wanted when the rest of us would have just given up. He even convinced me once to go to a restaurant and try Indian food when he knew I was still strictly a meat and potatoes kind of guy. I had adamantly refused to go when Gene asked me if I liked barbecued chicken. I had to admit I did like barbecued chicken, so off I went, against my better judgment to this Indian restaurant, the first one I had ever been to, and they ordered tandori chicken for me. The rest of the party ordered all kinds of smelly dishes while I filled up on chicken. Little did I know that I would come to love Indian food, even the smelly stuff, and I would have Gene Wasosky to thank for hauling me off to a restaurant that I wasn't really interested in.

It was at one of those October softball games, video Sundays, or restaurant outings, that Gene first broached the subject of a trip he was beginning to plan. The trip was to take place over our three week semester break in December. When he finally broached the question, it came as a complete shock to both my wife and me.

Would we be interested in a trip to visit a tribe of people who were still living in the Stone Age?

My first reaction was to wonder what the hell he was talking about. Here we were in October and he was talking about some trip in late December. My second reaction was to think seriously about accusing Gene of being a liar. There were no Stone Age people left in the world. Sure, I had heard of tribes in the Amazon rain forest that were living a very primitive existence, but I sure wasn't going to fly off to the Amazon rain forest to find them.

Gene assured me there was such a tribe and we wouldn't have to fly to South America to find them because they lived right here in Indonesia. Now I knew he was pulling my leg. There couldn't possibly be such a tribe in the country I was living in.

Gene explained that the tribe he was talking about lived in Irian Jaya, and were called the Dani tribe. He was going to organize a trip to visit them and my wife and I were invited to come along.

I had no clue where Irian Jaya was until he explained it was the western half of New Guinea, which was now a part of Indonesia.

At least I had heard of New Guinea. I knew that there had been fierce fighting in New Guinea between the Allies and the Japanese during World War II, but I really didn't know where it was located, how one got there from Jakarta, or why in the world we had to start thinking about going there when it was only October.

Gene explained that the trip would not be easy. There would be paper work to fill out just to get permission to go into the interior of Irian Jaya to a place called the Baliem Valley. We would have to get shots, take medicine to prevent malaria, logistics on what to pack for clothing and food, what to take in for trade items, and sleeping supplies. The lists went on and on. That, he said, is why we had to make the commitment now because it would take a lot of time to get everything together for this trip of a lifetime.

This was an awful lot to digest. Did we really want to make this trip? What would happen if we got really sick? Was this tribe dangerous? Were there poisonous snakes that might kill us if we got bitten? Were we putting ourselves in danger by going into such a primitive place with such primitive people?

We were given a few days to think about whether we were going to go ahead or decline participating in this grand adventure.

The more we thought about it the more intrigued we were with the idea. Who could say they had stepped back in time thousands of years? How many people would ever have this kind of an opportunity in their lifetime?

The nice thing about being young, and naïve, is you don't

really dwell on all of the things that could go wrong. You think only of the adventure, the experience, of being able to see something few others would ever be able to see.

Gene promised that there would be only six of us on the trip. The plane we would fly in on would not accommodate more than the six of us, our supplies, the pilot, a guide and a policeman who must accompany us.

My wife and I took a couple days to think about the offer. We didn't really know what we would be doing over our semester break and Gene Wasosky could be very persuasive. Gene assured us that he would be doing most of the planning. It sounded pretty simple to us, so after a short debate, we told Gene we were all in.

Now we could go back to teaching.

5

ORGANIZING THE TRIP TO IRIAN JAYA

Once we had committed to the trip we became a party of six. Kathy and Gene Wasosky would become the leads. Gene would do most of the legwork in Jakarta, and Kathy, with her art background would become the unofficial photographer. Gene and Kathy were friends with Art and Joan Dunn who were both elementary teachers at the school. Pam and I didn't know the Dunn's before agreeing to take part in this adventure into the interior of Irian Jaya but they turned out to be good people, more than willing to do their part in making sure the trip went as smoothly as possible.

We met several times as a group of six as the semester progressed with the hope of covering all of the logistics that would make the trip go off without a hitch. By this time all of us were fairly experienced travelers, and we realized you always make some mistakes when preparing for any trip. The preparations for this trip took on considerable more importance since there would be no Seven Eleven, no pharmacy, and no stores to go to if we ran into any unforeseen emergency on a trip. What we packed is what we would have available once we got to the Baliem Valley, so we had to plan for any eventualities we might encounter once we were on our own In Irian Jaya.

We decided to use a travel agent in Jakarta who would lay out the itinerary for the trip. If I recall correctly we met the travel agent, Sjam, (Indonesians often go by one name) on several different occasions. Sjam promised to have everything laid out in a timely manner so we could have the time we needed to take care of the many details necessary to carry out a trip of this nature.

One of the first orders of business she mentioned was our need to secure a "Jalan Surat." The literal translation for "Jalan Surat" is walking letter. Of course, we were curious why we would need a Jalan Surat. There was a pregnant pause, while Sjam seemed to be thinking how to explain what a Jalan Surat was, and why we would not be able to travel into the Baliem Valley without this crucial letter.

A Jalan Surat, she explained, simply allows you to travel to this very remote part of Indonesia. While saying all of this, she cast her eyes down, as Indonesians often do when they are nervous. When delivering unpleasant information Javanese don't like to look you directly in the eyes. They much prefer to make you happy by giving you pleasant information in which all parties can smile.

After much fidgeting, she finally said that the Indonesian government really wasn't all that keen on letting foreigners travel into Irian Jaya, and in particular, they were not happy if you were traveling into the Baliem Valley. She went on to say that the Indonesian government was somewhat ashamed of the Dani tribes. After all, they were a Stone Age tribal culture. They didn't wear Western clothes. They couldn't read. They couldn't write. They had no idea how old they were, how old their parents were, or even how old their children were. They only had wooden tools and stone axes. There were no metal instruments like knives or spears.

What would the rest of the world think if they learned how primitive the Dani people were? How would it affect the way the world viewed Indonesia?

Only then did she explain how expensive the Jalan Surat would be along with everything else that went into issuing the document.

Indonesia, at that time, was a very poor country. The average income was only a few hundred dollars a year. There was, however, an abundance of natural resources in the country. The country was rich in timber, gold, copper, and oil. Unfortunately these resources were controlled by the government and a few ultra rich families. The distribution of wealth was very unequal. The rich got richer, and the poor, the vast majority of the country, remained on a subsistence level.

Nothing is ever exactly as it seems in Indonesia. It is like peeling back the layers of an onion. Just when you think you understand how things work in the Indonesia, you peel back the outer layer of the onion only to find another layer beneath. No matter how many layers you peel back, there is still another layer. Were they really concerned what the rest of the world thought about their Stone Age citizens? Did they come up with this idea of a Jalan Surat to help people living Irian Jaya, or was this just another money grab to grease the palms of some people in power? Would Sjam be getting her cut in the issuance of the Jalan Surat? There was no real way of knowing the answer to these questions.

You peel back the outer layer and there is still another layer of the onion.

We had all lived in Indonesia long enough to understand it didn't make any difference what the reasoning was. If we didn't pay for the Jalan Surat, there was no way in hell we would ever be allowed to travel into the Baliem Valley and have our adventure of a lifetime with the Dani tribes.

So, of course, we paid. The cost of the trip just went up, but we really had no choice.

Sjam also made us aware, at this initial meeting, that we would not be the only six members of the trip. We would have a guide to accompany us, one who had experience dealing with expeditions into the valley. In addition to the guide, we would be required to take with us an Indonesian policeman. The policeman, we were told, was for our protection if anything went wrong on the trip. Sjam assured us that the policeman would have a gun, but not to worry, he in all likelihood would not have to use it. This really painted an amazing picture for us as Indonesia did not usually allow weapons, even for the police.

It was not a very reassuring thought for any of us, and I'm sure each of us wondered if we might be biting off more than we could chew. No one said anything. It made each of us a little nervous, but if anything, it increased our excitement about making the trip. My wife and I, both small town kids from rural Wisconsin, thought that a trip like this would be amazing.

Sjam said she would have a full itinerary out to us in a few weeks. She would detail each day, where we would be, what we would see, and in which village we would spend the night.

We left the meeting with adrenaline flowing through our veins and a sense of purpose of what we had to do to get ready for the trip.

We met several more times throughout first semester to go over the packing arrangement. What foods should we take? What clothes should we pack? What kind of a medical kit would be needed in case we were injured or sick? We knew we would not be able to drink the water, so we had to estimate how much liquid consumption six people would need during our stay? Plastic water bottles were not yet available in Indonesia at the time.

We finally decided we would have to forgo coffee on the trip so we packed tea bags. We took along Tang, the orange flavored drink. We also decided we would pack several cases of Seven Up in cans. Each person decided what snack items they would pack. We were told to plan on walking five to ten miles each day, so we would need some snacks to get us by between meals.

Rice would be our staple for meals and that would be an easy item to pack.

We were told by Sjam that we would be sleeping in different Dani villages and that Dani tribesmen do not sleep in beds. We would be sleeping in their huts, on the ground. We decided that sleeping bags were too heavy and cumbersome to take with us and carry from village to village so we agreed we would each buy two Indonesian sarongs, sew them together, and this would suffice as a sleeping sack.

What can I say? It seemed to make sense at the time.

We knew we needed enough supplies for the time we would be in the Baliem Valley but we didn't want the load to become too cumbersome to carry long distances.

We would take just enough clothes along to get us through the trip. We realized there would be no showers waiting for us in the valley, and I think in the back of our minds we had come to the conclusion that we would be wearing the same clothes day after day, with no chance for a bath.

We each took a small day pack to carry our snacks, sun glasses and glasses, cameras and film.

We also made plans to do some trading with the Dani tribes.

Gene, in particular, already had a large collection of primitive art. He was a serious collector and he was very much looking forward to coming back with as many examples of Dani art as he could. Sjam mentioned that the Dani tribes were just starting to move away from the barter system, which was the only trade system they had ever known. We were told not to be surprised if we got to a village and bartering for items would be the only form of trade they knew.

Money was just starting to trickle into Wamena, the only town in the valley. Wamena also held the only air strip in the valley. Sjam said that the Dani might recognize the 100 Rupiah note, which happened to be worth only pennies. They might accept payment in these red colored 100 Rupiah notes, but they wouldn't trade in other notes since they were a different color which they had not seen before.

Sjam did give us some suggestions of what to bring along to trade. She especially emphasized the Dani would be more comfortable dealing with barter items rather than money. All Dani men and women, she said, loved to smoke. They grew a type of tobacco but were open to any new tobacco that we might bring with us. Also, cigarettes could be used as a good will offering, a chance for us to show friendship and our good intentions. None of us were smokers, so we felt a little weird bringing in cigarettes. We knew they were bad for your health and it was an example of several ethical choices we had to make on the trip. In the end, we decided we were not there to change the Dani culture, so we packed a lot of cigarettes. Our guilt was eased when we were told that all Dani men smoked and they would love receiving tobacco.

We were told that a good trade item might be small mirrors, since they had never seen a mirror before. We ended up not taking the mirrors because we thought they would be broken before we had a chance to trade them, a decision we would later regret.

We were also asked to bring in several shovels to give to a couple of village chiefs. We didn't need to bring the wooden handles, just the shovel head would do. They would find their own wooden handles. It seemed bizarre to think the Dani's could go from the Stone Age to the Iron Age with something as simple as a shovel head.

A group of six teachers had made a trip to the Baliem Valley the previous year, so we would be the second set of teachers to make this journey. We checked with those teachers to get their suggestions and they were the ones who asked us to take along the shovels, something they had not done but in hindsight, thought would be useful. They had taken photos of several Dani chiefs and had the photos mounted on nice wood frames. Our friends asked us if we would take the framed photos with us to present to each chief. We placed the photos among the mounting items we were gathering for the trip.

We each started collecting our own supplies as the semester began winding down and our excitement for the upcoming trip began to climb.

The Jalan Surat had been procured, the plane tickets paid for, Sjam had come through with the daily itinerary for the trip in which she concluded each day's itinerary with this thought, "Follow the Happenings All Night Long."

We were really going to do this. This wasn't just a pipe dream any longer. We were off to visit the Dani tribes of Irian Jaya.

The time had arrived.

We were all packed and ready for the trip of a lifetime.

6

SET BACK

The first semester at Jakarta International School had come to a grinding halt and all of the teachers were looking forward to three glorious weeks without students, without papers to correct, without responsibilities to anyone but themselves. A comment we heard often from teachers at JIS was that teaching at Jakarta International School was like running as fast as you could on a treadmill. At the end of the semester, you were able to jump off the treadmill, go on vacation and decompress. I thought that was one of the reasons the school gave us a three week break between first and second semester; the administration realized how hard teachers worked when school was in session. They were also cognizant of the fact that we needed some extra time to recover from the hectic pace of the school so when we came back we would be refreshed, reinvigorated, and ready to jump back on the fast moving treadmill. After we returned, we would once again sprint like crazy until school year came to a grinding halt at the end of May.

It wasn't just teachers who needed a break. Much was expected of students who attended JIS. Competition in classes was fierce. All of the students were university bound. The percentage of our senior students who would be accepted to universities was nearly ninety-eight percent. Many of these students would attend prestigious universities scattered around the world. It was not uncommon for JIS graduates to be accepted at Ivy League colleges and universities in the States. We had students who would be accepted at Brown, Penn, Tufts, Carnegie Mellon, Stanford, Michigan, Boston College, just to name a few of the more popular colleges and universities in the States. Every few years one of our graduates would apply and gain acceptance into Harvard.

Those were just the U.S. bound universities. Many of our students would go back to their country of origin and matriculate to one of the fine institutions of higher learning in their native lands.

The point being, students needed to give their brains a break as much as the teachers needed to get away.

It was always interesting talking to students and teachers about what their plans were over the three weeks we would all be apart. Many of the students would stay in Indonesia, but spend much of their break in Bali. Bali was wonderful, inexpensive, and a paradise for students. Students could get a "losmen," a small thatched hut with a cold water tap, a couple of chairs, a bed with a sheet for covering, an overhead fan that made a feeble attempt to move the air around, and a lamp with a 40 watt bulb, all for $5.00 a night.

They would rent motor bikes and take their life in their hands as they sped down beaches or on narrow, congested roads. Motorbikes could be dangerous. There were times when one or more of our students would be pushed off the road by passing cars and end up in a hospital with serious injuries.

The students would spend their days snorkeling, surfing, or lying about in the sun, eating at cheap restaurants, and meeting up with other school friends to dance the night away at local clubs.

Some of the teachers would also spend most of their time in Bali. Both parties, students and teachers, hoped not to see each other. We all needed our own space. There was an unwritten rule that both students and teachers seemed to understand. If a teacher saw a student or if a student saw a teacher, each would take another route if possible, or overt their eyes if it wasn't. Teachers didn't want to see their sixteen year old students walking down the beach with a beer in one hand and a cigarette in the other. Students didn't want to see single teachers with their Indonesian girl friends or married teachers with their young children.

We would be happy to see each other and get caught up at the end of three glorious weeks of relaxing, but right now we just wanted to be away from Jakarta, the school, and each other.

The six of us, on the other hand, had other plans.

On December 22, 1980 we were off on our great adventure.

We were up at 2 a.m. after practically no sleep. We were both nervous and excited. Sleep was an afterthought. We were too keyed up at the prospect of going to Irian Jaya.

Burt Poulin, one of our teacher friends, picked us up at 2:45 a.m. to take us to Kamayoran airport, the airport in Jakarta used for domestic flights. We had never used this particular airport before and we were shocked to see it completely packed at 3:30 in the morning. Kretek cigarette smoke hung in the air, even at this ungodly hour.

We got in the wrong line and the only way to switch lines

was to push and shove. After two and a half years in Indonesia, we had become "Indonesianized." We now pushed and shoved just like the locals. I handed luggage over top of people, reached around them, and we somehow got everyone checked in.

The 5:00 a.m. flight time came and went, but this was Indonesia, nothing ever went on time, so we had few worries. At 6:30, ticket agents finally announced that the flight was not going off. We could get to Ujung Pandang, previously Makassar, in Sulawesi, but we could get no further. We hung our heads, recollected our luggage, got a couple of taxi's and went back home to catch five or six hours of sleep in the afternoon.

Our great adventure was not off to an auspicious start. We would have to wait another day with the hope our flight would not be cancelled again. We knew that in Indonesia nothing was ever guaranteed. Things did not run on time or on a regular basis. "Rubber time" was the term most often used in Indonesia. If you were to survive and prosper in Indonesia, you were forced to develop some patience. You could never be absolutely sure of anything running on schedule.

Tomorrow we would try again.

If all went well, tomorrow we would get out of Jakarta. None of us wanted to contemplate what would happen if our flights were delayed a second time.

7

LET'S TRY AGAIN

The taxi dropped us off at our house and we went to
bed to catch up on the sleep we had missed the previous night.
We slept for a few hours into the afternoon, got up, showered,
and took a walk around our housing complex in Pondok Indah.
We tried to regroup, calm our emotions, and prepare for a

flight we hoped would happen the next morning. If all went well, if we connected with our different flights, we would be in Jayapura, Irian Jaya the next evening.

We had our evening meal, perhaps the last good meal we would have for a number of days, and went back to bed.

Sleep escaped us. We were up by 1:30 a.m. because none of the intrepid six was positive we were registered in the computer since our flight had been cancelled the previous morning. This was Indonesia. Stuff happened all the time that made no sense to our western trained minds. We had heard too many horror stories of flight problems, people being stranded for days before they could sort out alternative plans to get where they wanted to go or get back from where they had been.

In Indonesia, you learn quickly you are never on your way to your destination until you are on the airplane, taxiing down the runway with the plane lifting off the tarmac.

We arrived at a less crowded Kamayoran airport at 2:30 a.m., found the correct check-in line on our first attempt and got our luggage checked through without incident. So far, we were making more progress than we had the previous morning.

The plane was on the tarmac, and we watched as our luggage got loaded aboard.

The flight actually took off on time, we settled into our seats, and we were soon jetting off to Ujung Pandang, Sulawesi, which previously had been called the Celebes.

We landed in Ujung Pandang and got right back on another plane that flew to the island of Ambon. From Ambon we flew across the Molucca Sea and landed on the island of Biak. From Biak it was a relatively short flight to Jayapura, Irian Jaya. The air miles we'd covered added up to a little over 2,700 miles. We had made it. We were now one short flight away from the

Baliem Valley and the Dani tribe we had been dreaming about. We were now only 160 air miles away from our arrival in Wamena.

We were met at the airport by our guide, Rudolf Willem, who was to accompany us into the Baliem Valley. Willem was a Dutch name. Dutch names were still common in Indonesia because of the Dutch influence on the country during the time they controlled Indonesia.

Rudolf Willem was part Sulawesian and part Javanese. We were made aware that he spoke six languages either fluently, or at least enough to get along. He looked like a used car salesman but he would turn out to be an excellent guide. He was knowledgeable, accommodating, and he had a ton of stories that he was more than willing to share with us. He and Sjam were either related by blood, or had a working relationship with each other for years. Nepotism was common in Indonesia and you could never be sure what connections one person might have with another.

The countryside around Jayapura was very rugged, with a number of streams and rivers. We looked across at Lake Sentani, a large freshwater lake between the airstrip and the town of Jayapura.

Jayapura was by no means a beautiful city. It was rundown and dirty. It looked like a city that desperately needed a good scrubbing and a new paint job on many of the buildings. It is a seaport city with many ships dotting the horizon. The ships that were docked were offloading their cargoes while bilges pumped out dirty water. The water was covered with oil slicks and garbage.

The city had a hard edge about it, a used edge. If it ever had a golden age, that time period was now passed.

We were loaded into taxis and taken to our hotel where we would spend a night before boarding a small plane for our trip to Wamena, the only town in the Baliem Valley. The hotel supported our initial impression of the city. It was old, dingy, and appeared to have never been updated since it had been built.

We didn't care. We had lost a day of the trip but we were now where we wanted to be. Tomorrow would be December 24, Christmas Eve day, and if our luck held we would be off to our final destination.

We went out for a very forgettable meal, crawled into bed, and tried to catch up on as much sleep as we could.

Tomorrow would be a very big day in all of our lives.

8

FLIGHT TO WAMENA

We were up early once again in anticipation of our flight to Wamena. There was a lot of nervous energy amongst all of us as we sat down at 7:30 for our last breakfast before boarding a plane that would take us on our last leg of the journey into the Baliem Valley.

We had all gone to bed the night before worrying about the weather. Sjam had given us an awful lot of information about the trip, preparations that had to be made, paperwork that had to be filled out, and ideas for packing. She had given us an itinerary for each day we would be in the valley, where we would be on any given day, what village we would be visiting, and what we could expect to see once we got there.

What she had forgotten to mention is that it might not be possible to fly into the Baliem Valley at all. We were scheduled to fly into Wamena on an Otter plane that carried up to 14 passengers. The flight from Jayapura to Wamena would take approximately one hour. We would have the plane to ourselves, along with Rudolf Willem, the pilot, and the policeman that was required to accompany us.

The plane, we found out, would have no instrumentation. We would be flying blind. If the weather was rainy, if turbulence became a factor, we wouldn't be able to fly at all. The weather forecast had to be clear all the way to Wamena because we would be flying over extremely rugged jungle terrain with winding, muddy rivers. There were mountains in Irian Jaya that were as high as 10,000 feet. Without visual confirmation, the plane could fly into one of those high mountains. Until we got to Wamena there would be no roads, no landing strips, and certainly no way of getting help if the plane were to have mechanical failure. Weather conditions could change quickly in this mountainous jungle area. If the skies were not clear, if safety was a concern, then the flight would be cancelled.

This was unexpectedly bad news. We had already lost a day of the planned trip due to the flight cancellation in Jakarta, so we certainly didn't want to lose any more time. We had all lived in Indonesia long enough to know that sometimes you aren't given all the facts. There are times when details that westerners are used to receiving are conveniently left out. Indonesians like to please, so they sometimes omit information that might displease you. This lack of transparency is simply a part of Indonesian culture.

Our luck seemed to have finally changed as we looked out on the early morning sun shining bright and clear. Our guide,

Rudolf, informed us that everything was a go, the plane was ready, the weather reports indicated that the sky would be clear all the way to Wamena, and we would be off after breakfast.

We ate a quick, forgettable breakfast, grabbed our gear, loaded into a van and headed back to the airport. Even though it was a domestic flight, we still had to check in two full hours before the flight was scheduled for departure.

At 11:00 the plane was packed with all our gear, we were all seated, 6 teachers, a pilot, Rudolf our guide, and the policeman who had been assigned to accompany us. The policeman appeared in blue jeans, a T-shirt, and a black cowboy hat with a Playboy Bunny symbol on the side of it. This was the man who supposedly had a gun and was there to protect us if anything went terribly array.

Was he really a policeman, a relative of Sjam, or was he a friend of Rudolf Willem? In Indonesia there is a philosophy of shared poverty. If a family, or relative, has a job then they have an obligation to help their immediate family out financially or at least help them obtain a job. Under this philosophy Indonesians end up sharing the poverty the country imposes upon them. It is a concept that the western mind finds hard to understand, but it is a large part of the social fabric of Indonesia.

Once you have lived in Indonesia for a few years, you think you understand the culture of the country. Remember, if you peel back a layer of the onion, you will find another layer underneath. We were foreigners and we would never understand the Indonesian culture completely. Nothing in Indonesian culture is exactly as it seems.

All we knew for sure was that we were packed into this small Otter aircraft and we were taxiing down the runway ready to lift off. We saw the land slip away beneath us as we left Jayapura behind. We were all prepared for the one hour flight to Wamena, and equally prepared for our great adventure to begin in a valley that was only 80 kilometers long and 20 kilometers wide.

It took only a few minutes before we had left the modern world behind. We were now flying over jungle terrain so thick our eyes could not penetrate the landscape below. The Otter continued to climb, gaining elevation as mountains jutted up before us, each seemingly higher than the previous one. We were all excited, craning to look out windows, anxious not to miss the impenetrable landscape below.

The only thing we were able to see was an ever expanding greenery of flora and jungle canopy. The only other visible landmark was the meandering brown rivers snaking through that greenery. No matter where you looked below, there was no separation in the jungle. The jungle seemed to be one continuous mass of green. There were no villages carved out of the jungle that were visible to us, not even a crude road etched into the landscape. There was simply mile after mile of green and brown. No wonder clear skies were needed in order to make the flight from Jayapura to Wamena. We knew somewhere below us, under the canopy of green, there were life forces, both animal and human, but they were beyond the scope of our human eyes.

I think we all realized, as we looked down on the jungle below, that if there was mechanical trouble on the aircraft, if we were forced to ditch in the jungle, not only would we die, but in all likelihood our bodies and the plane would never be located. We would simply be swallowed up by the jungle.

It is not that we were overly concerned by this possibility; it simply seemed to be the reality of where we were and where we were headed.

The flight was smooth, there were no winds, and we

travelled through a smattering of fluffy white clouds. We were heading into an area of the world that was untamed, seemingly untamable.

Time ticked by. We flew over some of the highest peaks and suddenly we could see village compounds below us. We could see clearly, round, thatched huts, built in concentric circles with wooden fences connected one hut to the next. We were not just viewing a circle of houses, it seemed as though we were viewing the circle of village life that had not changed in millennium.

Cameras were out and photos were quickly snapped. Those first photos were our attempt to capture on film what we were unable to put into words.

The airstrip lay before us as we descended down through scattered clouds. At the end of the runway, we could see Wamena in the distance. It was a small town of tin roofs and small wood-sided houses. No roads could be seen leading out of town, only worn paths of dirt and rock.

We saw our first Dani tribesmen before we ever touched down, slender men dressed only in a penis gourd called a koteka. They were stoic figures, eyes cast upward to the heavens, viewing the future descending towards them.

We deplaned and collected our belongings. Several of the Dani men had come to Wamena to assist us. They walked towards us, smiles spread across their faces, a small welcoming committee of men with bare chests covered in pig's grease.

We looked at these Dani men, their bodies glistening dark in the sunlight from the pigs grease they rubbed on their bodies, kotekas standing erect, held aloft by two woven strings.

They smiled.

We smiled.

They picked up some of our luggage and herded us to a spot where lunch was already being prepared.

The lunch consisted of rice, chicken, and vegetables. After we had had our fill of food we wandered though the small town. The roads in town were narrow and dirt covered. We found the town market where items were brought in to trade. We saw vegetables, head dresses, and plugs of tobacco that would be bartered away before the day was done. The pillars of the market were covered with pigs grease. There were hand and arm prints where Dani men and women had leaned against them, or reached up to rest an arm. Flies were abundant, landing on rotting rubbish and humans in equal measure.

As we walked around a small portion of Wamena, we were surprised to see a Xerox sign outside one of the huts. It was hanging on the side of a small building, unused, and in disrepair. Yet it was there, a sign of the encroachment of the modern world. It was so out of place that we all laughed when we saw it. It got all of us thinking about how Wamena ever got started as a town in the first place. One of us asked our guide why Wamena even existed. Who had created Wamena, and for what purpose? Rudolf explained that the Indonesian government had developed the town and the landing strip. The reason Wamena exists, he explained, is that the Indonesian government was exploring Irian Jaya for mineral deposits and they needed a place to land planes, set up some offices, and a central location to stake out their right to start prospecting for mineral deposits.

That explained the Xerox sign. They would have to copy documents related to their search for mineral deposits.

Where had they searched? What had they found? Where were they going next to search for riches?

We found it astonishing that Wamena was never set up to help the Dani tribes in any way. It was simply a jumping off point for the sole purpose of enriching the Indonesian government.

We spent thirty minutes wandering around a very small market, taking photos before collecting our belongings, heading out of town, and starting our first trek. According to our itinerary, we would have a two hour walk to the first village we were to visit. The name of the village we were walking to was a place called Aikima.

We walked across a bridge and were soon on our way. The weather was hot, hats and sunglasses came out and water bottles got opened and sipped. As soon as we left Wamena, we found ourselves walking over rough paths made of stone and dirt. From this point on, there would be no roads; simple worn paths of rock and dirt would take us on our journey. Our two Dani hosts walked with us. They had bare feet that were wide and splayed, with calluses about a half inch thick. We could feel the stones pushing up beneath our good walking shoes, but the Dani porters showed no sign of pain, or discomfort, as they carried part of our gear hoisted high on their shoulders.

The town of Wamena was left behind, soon becoming a dwindling image as our small entourage trudged on in the mid-day sun toward the village of Aikima.

9

THE MUMMY OF AIKIMA

As we walked towards Aikima, we couldn't help noticing the well maintained garden plots along the way. Each garden was clearly delineated from the next. Each garden had irrigation ditches that were filled with water. We learned that about ninety percent of the Dani diet comes from sweet potatoes. Sweet potatoes are not the easiest vegetable to grow. For proper growth, they need a certain amount of water on a regular basis. The irrigation ditches were a necessity, especially when there was a lack of rainfall.

This is where the Dani also grow gourds, ginger, taro, cucumbers, yams, greens, and carrots, yet it is the sweet potato that is essential for Dani life. Sweet potatoes are eaten each day and the Dani have names for seventy different types of sweet potatoes. Their diet is limited, changes little from day to day, and is high in starch and light in protein.

Gardens are ongoing, each family owning multiple gardens which are staggered for planting at different times. As one garden is harvested another is ready to start producing, and another is ready to be planted.

As the fields are cleared for planting, the excess grass and plants are heaped on the gardens. This grass and plants rot as irrigated water is poured on the garden. Once the sweet potatoes and other vegetables are harvested, pigs are brought in to forage through the rotting vegetation to eat any sweet potatoes that were missed when the potatoes were dug up.

As we walked along worn paths, we would see women working in the fields, white egrets were standing erect near the irrigation ditches, daily Dani life unfolding before us.

We watched as Dani men and women would meet each other along the paths. The women might be coming out of the fields, the men going or coming from a morning trip to Wamena, or from a visit to another Dani village.

No man or woman was left without first being greeted. You immediately become impressed with the friendliness and openness of the Dani people. The Dani have a warm and gentle way of greeting each other. They will embrace, forearm to forearm, bodies touching, speaking in very gentle voices. We learned quickly that "wha, wha, wha" is a sign of happiness and endearment when they meet someone they know well. We saw these same greetings play out before us day after day and still marveled at the kindness and friendliness shown towards one another.

It is difficult to imagine these gentle souls are just a few years removed from ritual wars, intent on killing or maiming, gaining land and territory from their enemies. They used revenge killings to appease the ghosts of their ancestors who had been killed or maimed by their enemies.

We walked on as more greetings were exchanged between men and women until we finally reached the village of Aikima. We entered the compound and saw our first Dani houses from ground level. The houses are called honai. They are cylindrical in shape with thatched roofs made of long grass. They are not tall structures, perhaps no higher than eight feet, with a few more prominent honai being higher than that. They are usually only one story, but they can be as high as two stories. The one entrance to the honai is a small opening, more of a crawl space than a doorway. The wooden sides of the honai are lashed together by vines and each honai is attached to the next honai by short wooden planks.

We were greeted by the village chief who ended up being a real ham. He insisted on having his photo taken with all the women and he made fun of all of us. You don't need to speak the language to understand joy and laughter. Some people just have a twinkle in their eye and a way of teasing that is universally understood.

Sjam had written in the itinerary that we would meet a famous chief in this village. We thought we must be looking at him, since this man with the twinkle in his eye was clearly the chief of Aikima. When we mentioned this, the chief laughed and told us he was not the famous chief, although he was the current chief.

The famous chief, we were told, was in his honai, but before we could see him we had to pay a small tribute of money. A few Indonesian bills were laid on the ground and the chief turned to a couple of the tribesmen who scurried off to the honai to retrieve the chief who really was famous.

The tribesmen came out of the honai carrying a chair. On the chair was something black, but we couldn't make out what it was. As the chair came closer, our eyes began to focus on the object being carried in the chair. The occupant of the chair was in a sitting position with his head bowed. We soon realized that the chief was never going to get out of this sitting position because he had been mummified. More precisely, he had been smoked. There was almost no flesh left on his bones.

We kept staring at this mummified man and I don't think any of us knew exactly what to say.

The current chief explained, through Rudolf Willem, that the chief was 400 years old, and apparently a fine leader of men. When he died, the village decided to preserve him and the only way to do that was to smoke him, which they did.

The Dani have no concept of time or age. They can't read, write, nor do any of them even know how old they are. How an assessment of the age of this mummified chief got established, was never satisfactorily answered. All we knew for sure was he was definitely dead, and had been for a very long time. Time had indeed taken a toll on the body. Part of the head had deteriorated over many years and the rest of the body showed the wear and tear of being exposed to the tropical heat.

We snapped some photos of the mummy before the chief was once again returned to his place of honor in the honai, still sitting silently in his chair. Recent research mentions that this famous chief is still paraded out to visitors who offer a few rupiah notes for the privilege of viewing the mummified Chief of Aikima

We didn't bother to wave good-bye to the mummy, and he didn't bother to wave to us.

We all sort of stared at each other as if to say, "Well, that was interesting."

We walked around the village of Aikima and took more photos. We noticed how each honai was attached to the next with a small wooden fence. There were certain places where the fence could be opened and closed. We would learn that the pigs, the most valuable possessions of the Dani, would be locked inside the village at night and then let out of the wooden gates in the morning to forage for food.

We still had one and a half hours of walking ahead of us. We were given bananas to eat before we departed and then we were on the path again, our Dani porters leading the way out of Aikima. We started our trek once more, heading to the village of Wiyagoba.

After we had walked an hour, we were met by Killian, Chief of Wiyagoba, and his wife, who accompanied us the last half hour until we arrived at his village.

We were tired after a long but eventful day. We had taken a small plane over dense jungle to get to Wamena, had been greeted by men wearing only penis gourds, had seen a Xerox sign where one never should have been, and had met a great chief who had been so beloved that the village had him mummified.

We had no idea what we would see next, but it would be hard to top what we had just seen in our first day in the land of the Dani.

What could possibly top seeing a mummified chief?

If we only knew then some of things that we were about to be exposed to in the next few days, we would have had to reevaluate our assessment that the mummy would be the highlight of the trip.

10

KILLIAN, CHIEF OF WIYAGOBA VILLAGE

How do I describe Killian, Chief of Wiyagoba Village? He was a most impressive visage of a man. He had a broad chest and a chiseled frame. His body fat was almost nonexistent due to the lack of sugar in the Dani diet. He had a broad smile that displayed all of his seemingly perfect teeth. He smiled readily and never seemed to be in a dour mood. Killian was not a tall man, perhaps just a shade less than six feet from head to toe, yet when you were in his presence you felt as though it was you who were the shorter person. His feet, like all Dani men and women, are wide and flat from spending his entire life without shoes. He was covered head to toe in thick pig's grease, which the Dani believe helps keep body heat in during the cold nights.

If these were the entire characteristics of Killian you would say he was a fine specimen of a man, but that would short change the image he projected. If you didn't know who the chief of Wiyagoba Village was and someone asked you to make a guess who you thought the village chief might be, Killian would no doubt be the first man you would pick. You would look at the men of the village and say, "That one there, that one must surely be the chief of this village."

Killian had an aura about him, a presence, a dignity, intelligence. If you lived in this village, he would be the man whom you would want as your leader.

If you had to guess his age, always a tough thing to do in the tropics where people tend to age rather quickly, you would guess him to be somewhere between thirty-five and forty years old. Due to being out in the tropical sun each day without sun screen, or even a hat, the skin becomes crinkled around the eyes from squinting. Someone can look much older than their chronological years.

Killian, we would learn, had one other unique characteristic. Although he was the Chief of Wiyagoba Village, he had only one wife. We would find out that this was very rare for a chief to have only one wife since polygamy was common, and Killian could easily have purchased other wives. The purchase price of a wife would be a few pigs, the most valuable currency of any Dani man.

Not only did Killian have only one wife, he seemed to be quite fond of her. Killian's wife seemed almost omnipresent when we were in Wiyagoba Village, whereas most Dani women were shy and reticent to interact with us.

When we met Killian on our way to his village, he was wearing a headband with many protruding feathers, a penis gourd, and dried pigs gonads around his elbows.

We continued to be impressed with how gentle and friendly the Dani were. We had to cross ditches and streams with a downed tree serving as the only means of crossing. The Dani porters were always there, taking the hands of our wives, guiding them across. If we crossed a boggy area of water and mud, porters would lay down a log or slab of wood. The Dani would stand in the mud up to their calves and help guide each woman across safely.

It is strange to see these powerfully built people be so gentle with one another. It is also strange to think that just a few years earlier they were still warring against enemy encroachment on their land. When attacked, they would use counter attacks, attempting to maim or kill their enemies to appease their ancestral ghosts.

It is even stranger to think that their greatest wish was to return to these warring days which had been officially banned by the Indonesian government in 1965.

By the time we got to Wiyagoba Village, we had been walking for at least four hours and had probably covered ten to twelve miles. We were tired, thirsty and hungry, yet filled with awe as to where we were and what we had already seen.

We were seated just outside the village compound, slabs of wood had been placed on the ground for us to sit on, and the village men had brought out trade items to barter. There were crude bows about four feet in length, arrows without fletching that were longer than their bows. The string of the bows was a narrow strip of bamboo that had been cured, stretched from end to end of the bow and tied off to create a taut bow string. The arrows had a notch cut in the end of the arrow that would just fit over the bow string.

There were spears with tips made from the toe of a cassowary bird. There were crude knives from sharpened cassowary bones, head nets that the women used for field work, breast plates made from small shells, feathered head dresses, bones from wild pigs made into fierce chest ornaments, and wild pig's tusks. The Dani would punch out the septum of their nose and place the pig's tusks through the septum to make them look even fiercer than they already were.

We were all anxious to buy, barter, or trade so we ran around like school children, afraid we might be left out of something we really wanted. It reminded me of Christmas shopping in the states where shoppers rush to buy that one special present before the store runs out. At the same time we were cognizant of the fact we were about as far removed from the civilized world as one could get.

We needn't have worried. Each village we visited had items for trade and we all left with pretty much everything on our wish list.

We weren't sure what to offer for any item, not wanting to offend our hosts. In Wiyagoba Village, most of the men would accept 100 Rupiah notes, but they were just as happy to bargain for a T-shirt, a hat, or anything else we had as a bargaining chip. I don't think it really made any difference to them. This was a social occasion for them as much as it was a trading session.

We plied them with Kretek cigarettes, which we had brought along in abundance. This pleased them as much as anything else we gave them. All adult Dani men and women smoke. I had never seen a people who enjoyed smoking as much as the Dani tribe. I think they would have gladly bartered items simply for the cigarettes we gave them. I really don't think they had a clue what the money was worth, nor did they particularly care. They were happy to enjoy a day that wasn't ordinary for them just as we were enjoying a day that certainly wasn't ordinary for us.

One of the most fascinating things about the trip, was that the Dani seemed as genuinely interested in us as we were with them.

The sun was waning, going down fast as it does in the tropics, with us visitors seated on a board plank on the ground. Killian was seated on one side of me, another Dani on the other, our shoulders touching. Insects were buzzing around my head, crawling over me as I shared with Killian the beef jerky I had brought along.

Killian, with a perpetual smile on his face, seemed to enjoy the jerky. It was a rare opportunity for him to get a little extra protein in his diet.

I was reminded yet again how unreal this whole experience was. I was in one of the most remote, undeveloped places on earth, surrounded by Stone Age tribesmen. This place, I thought, is surreal. I couldn't believe I was here, in this primitive setting, sitting alongside Dani warriors.

We had already seen so much on this our first day in the Baliem Valley. Our minds could only conjure up what we might see, or do, next.

We had a dinner of rice, potatoes, vegetables and soup. Soon after dinner, a chief of a neighboring village showed up at camp. He had a very long name that was impossible to say, and completely impossible to remember. His name started out as Wali before it became elongated into something indecipherable. We quickly adapted, shortened his name, and thereafter referred to him simply as Wali.

We also got tired of saying Rudolf Willem, so we just started calling him Willem. It seemed to fit him better than Rudolf.

Wali was an unimposing man, skinny of frame and stature, but, as it turned out, looks can be deceiving. Wali was one of the famous warriors of the Dani warring years. He had lead raids on enemy villages, been involved in wars, shot at enemies, and in turn, been shot at by enemies.

He and Killian were good friends, although Wali had to be at least twenty or thirty years older than Killian.

We would spend more time with these two chiefs than anyone else we were to meet in the valley, but it wasn't until later, that we would learn of Wali's greatest secret.

11

HONAI

The honai are the Dani houses. A typical village
would usually have less than one hundred inhabitants. There
were separate houses for the men and the women. The three
women in our group got special dispensation and were allowed
to sleep in the men's honai. This is something a Dani woman
would never be allowed to do.

A typical honai is a single story structure build with wood
construction. The wood only extends up about four feet and

there was a small crawl space as an entrance. The roof is made of thatched grass that extends down to the wood sides.

Each honai is attached to the next in a circular fashion by short wooden fencing. Each village creates an enclosed circle. There are one or two gates where people can enter or leave the compound.

You either bend or crawl into a honai. Once inside the honai there is little light that penetrates. It is a bit like being in a smoke house. Grass is spread across the earthen honai floor.

In the center of the honai, is a fire pit hacked into the earth. There is only a short entrance before you are inside of the honai. There is little air movement once you are inside the honai because of the fire in the pit. There is no place for the smoke to go once a fire is started because there are no windows in a honai. The Dani suffer from lung problems because they are constantly breathing in smoke from the fire pit. Being uneducated, they do not realize the smoke causes these lung problems.

The Baliem Valley sits in a bowl at an elevation of approximately 1,700 meters. The days are warm with temperatures reaching into the 80's and 90's, but once the sun goes down the temperatures drop quickly. The fires in the honai are necessary to keep as much heat in the honai as possible.

The women have their own honai. The wives of the chief may have more than one honai, depending on how many wives the chief has.

Each village has a long house which also serves as the cooking area of the women. The pigs also stay in this long house at night. We were warned not to go into the long houses because they are all infested with lice. That is all the convincing it took for us to give the long houses a wide berth.

You always make some mistakes when planning a trip. Our

biggest mistake was the use of sarongs sewn together to form a sleeping sack. We crawled into our sleeping sacks that first night, tired from our long walk. The fire in the pit was still burning as we tried to find a comfortable location on the grass covered floor. We tried to sleep but the ground was mighty hard when there was only a thin piece of cloth between you and mother earth. The sarongs were not long enough to cover our entire body. We had to bend our knees and scrunch up as best we could, which didn't prove to be all that comfortable.

The Dani on the other hand sleep in a sitting position with their backs against the honai walls, crossing their arms around their knees.

I woke that first night after only a few fitful minutes of sleep. I opened my eyes and all I could see were the whites of the Dani eyes staring back at me. Those stares were unnerving and it became difficult to drift back to sleep.

What we were totally unprepared for were the mosquitoes. The mosquitoes wanting out of the cold night air would fly into the honai and line up on the walls. I got dive bombed so many times I finally turned on my flashlight and I saw thousands of mosquitoes lined up like miniature bombers on the wooden walls. The only way you could sleep was to scrunch down and pull all of the sleeping sack around you. After fifteen or twenty minutes, claustrophobia would set in and you would have to come up for air. When you did that, the mosquitoes would feast on you until you once again fully covered your body. We got cold each night, bitten badly by mosquitoes.

The Dani, however, slept on. Did the pigs grease protect them from the mosquitoes or were they just immune to their bites? How did they stay warm once the fires went out?

The Dani were well adapted to their environment. We were not. They slept in a circle with their back against the wooden walls. We slept fitfully, waking frequently, adjusting and readjusting our sleeping sacks, but never becoming comfortable. We woke each morning a little more sleep deprived.

The Dani would be up before us and have a fire going in the courtyard. The warmth was greatly appreciated after the chill of the night. The women would have a bunch of fifty or more bananas roasting in the fire for their morning breakfast.

In the time we were in the Baliem Valley, I don't think we ever got more than a few hours sleep a night.

12

WALKING TO THE MOON

About now you are probably wondering how we communicated with the Dani. We, of course, had never learned Dani. The Dani, on the other hand, had never learned English.

Would this create an insurmountable barrier to communication?

During our first 24 hours after our arrival in the Baliem Valley, we had already picked up a few words of Dani. We learned the expression "wha, wha, wha," which was used to indicate happiness or endearment. We learned that "narok," or in some places in the valley "nayak" was a greeting by males to other males. It meant hello, good-bye and thank you.

If a man was greeting a woman he would say, "Laoak."

When women were addressing other women, they would always say "laoak."

It was fine to learn those few words but our limited vocabulary wasn't going to get us very far.

Communication became a fairly simple, yet long process. Missionaries had taught a few of our Dani helpers Bahasa Indonesian, the official language of Indonesia. We could ask a question in English, Willem could translate our English question to Bahasa. Heli and Yacoom, the two Dani interpreters who had learned Bahasa Indonesian would then translate Bahasa into Dani. When the Dani answered our questions the process would be reversed from Dani, to Bahasa, to English. This pretty much solved the communication gap, but the process of going through all of these language changes took time. We would ask a question, but by the time all the language translations took place it might be several minutes before we got a response we could understand.

Thankfully, the Dani seem to be a very patient people. Time was a relative concept to them, so it didn't bother them that this process of communication between English, Bahasa, and Dani was such a laborious process. They liked to talk, so time became a non-factor. In fact, they seemed to be just as interested in asking us questions as we were in asking questions of them.

One of the questions that seemed to really interest them is why we had come to see them in the first place. They hadn't seen many white people before and they had been taught by valley missionaries that their culture was very backward as compared to the rest of the world.

Why would we come to see such a primitive people? People who did not wear much for clothing, people whose wealth depended on the number of pigs they owned, people who had no formal education, who could neither read nor write, people who didn't even know how old they were?

We had to think about that for a minute until Gene Wasosky finally came up with an appropriate answer.

He explained that we were teachers, and as such, it was our job to study different cultures so we could go back and teach others about the Dani culture. Their culture was certainly unique and we had come to the Baliem Valley to learn from them.

This answer seemed to please them and the topic was never raised again. In fact, we were learning from them. They had a wealth of knowledge to share. We were learning a few words of Dani, we were learning that these were bright people, good farmers, fierce warriors, that pigs represented wealth, that they were warm and gentle with each other.

We had talked with Killian and Wali in Killian's honai late into the evening asking questions. Our brains finally became frazzled and we couldn't think of anything else to ask. We had temporarily run out of questions and were just coming out of the honai when we looked up and saw a full moon. One of us, I forget who, asked the two chiefs if they knew that man had walked on the moon? The question went through the multiple translation process as Killian and Wali kept looking up at the moon. They had an animated discussion back and forth, looking up at the moon often, before the answer finally got translated back to us. "No," they said, "they did not know that man had walked on the moon, but it really didn't matter to them because the moon was too far away. They would never be able to make it that far."

What they said next wasn't about walking to the moon, but they said it was a much greater wish than that. They desperately want to fly on an airplane. The Dani word for airplane was, "flying canoe."

They had heard about the city of Jayapura, home to more

people than they could ever imagine. They had also heard about big boats that swam on the water. They wanted to see one of these giant boats with their own eyes.

They had also heard about beds, and they wanted to try sleeping in a real bed instead of the sitting position against a honai wall that the Dani used for sleeping.

This was the first we had heard about their dream to fly to Jayapura, but it certainly wasn't going to be the last we heard of it. They would bring up this wish throughout our time in the valley. Wishes to fly on a plane, visit a city, see big boats and sleep in a real bed. They said they couldn't sleep at night thinking of such a trip. They compared it to waiting for your new wife on your wedding night.

Willem had promised them that someday soon he would take them to Jayapura on the same plane we had arrived on. They had promised Willem they would take a bath and wear real clothes when they made their journey of a lifetime because they didn't want to look any different than anyone else. They had pride, and they did not want to be stared at, or made fun of, because, as they said, they knew they were primitive.

I knew as I heard those words spoken that I would have paid a lot of money to be on that plane with Killian and Wali when they made their fateful journey. If I were able to go along, I wouldn't look at the canopy below me, wouldn't look at the brown, muddy rivers meandering through the jungle. I would not have taken my eyes off Killian and Wali the whole flight as they saw another world open up before them.

I could only imagine how wide their eyes would be, and the conversations they would have about zooming through the air in the flying canoe.

What Willem did not tell them was that this flight would be coming much sooner than the two chiefs thought. He was flying back into the valley in a couple of months and it would be on that trip that he would take Killian and Wali with him on their dream journey.

I was sad because I knew I wasn't going to be able fly with them, to see their eyes light up like children.

I never went on that flight, but I have certainly thought about it, then, and now.

I still think about it today, all these years later.

I hope their flight was an enjoyable one. I hope the flying canoe ride was everything they had dreamed it would be; like waiting for your new wife on your wedding night. I hope they saw the big ships, the cars, trucks and cranes, the hustle and bustle of a large city. I hope the day they made the trip to Jayapura the skies were blue, the landscape green, and they never encountered any turbulence along the way.

If their trip of a lifetime turned out to be as good as our trip into the Baliem Valley . . . well . . . no one could ask for a better trip than that.

13

NOT A PLACE TO BE BORN FEMALE

The year was 1938, and Richard Archbold, a 31 year old American pilot and zoologist, was on his third expedition to New Guinea looking for new discoveries. He was independently wealthy, a philanthropist, and a man who was financially sponsoring his own expedition.

The plane he was using, a PBY-2 Catalina Flying boat, was being piloted by Russell R. Rogers. The PBY-2 was chosen because it could land on rivers or lakes. It could be used for landing supplies, taking photographs, and transporting men for logistical support.

The PBY-2 was flying over some of the highest peaks in New

Guinea on June 23, 1938, when it descended upon a valley. Imagine his surprise when he looked down on well manicured gardens, irrigation ditches for collecting rainwater, and women working in those gardens. The women wore only a skirt made of orchid reeds.

The Archbold expedition had inadvertently made the discovery of a century. Archbold would soon introduce the world to the Dani people of the Baliem Valley, a primitive tribe who had not dramatically changed their culture in 50,000 years. One of the Dutch helpers quickly came up with the name, Grand Valley, to describe what they had just discovered.

The people that Archbold viewed from the air were living as pre-historic man had lived, unencumbered by civilization. He would discover that the Dani did not make pottery, had no metal tools, and had little knowledge of the outside world.

When we arrived in the Baliem Valley it had been just over 40 years since the Dani tribe had been introduced to the world. The outside world was slowly encroaching on the Dani tribe in 1980, but it was still encroaching at a glacial pace. We had arrived at a time when the confluences of those changes were just beginning to merge.

The words you are about to read regarding the women of the Dani tribes might make you uncomfortable. We had not come to the Baliem Valley to pass on our biases. We were in the Baliem Valley to visit, to listen, and learn from the Dani.

That said, you might find it hard to comprehend the lives of the Dani women. Their work, their marriages, their social status were much different than that of the Dani men. After you read these descriptions of the lives of females in the Dani tribes, you might better comprehend why the Baliem Valley was not a place to be born female, at least not from the Western World perspective.

The first women we saw on our walk out from the town of

Wamena were working in gardens. They wore only a skirt of orchid fibers which marked them as unmarried. They were naked from the waist up, their skin darkened from daily work in the tropical sun. They carried a sharpened stick for digging and they had "noken," on top of their heads. Noken were woven nets used for carrying everything from the sweet potatoes and the greens they harvested to small children who lay nestled in the noken, asleep, blissfully unaware of the strange white folks passing by. We would learn that social status for Dani women was dependent on the number of noken they owned. Each noken would be piled high on their head, a status symbol as to their standing in the village.

There wasn't a zaftig body among any of the women we saw in the valley, although the stomachs of both the women and the children were slightly protruded, we later learned was caused by the lack of protein in their diet. When pigs were slaughtered for ceremonial festivals, it was the grown men who ate most of the meat from the pigs. The women and offspring got very little of that delicacy, and only then the scraps left over after the men had eaten.

The Dani marry at a young age. Typically for girls it was around the age of 12, or about the time of puberty. Men married later, around the age of 18. Polygamy was common among the Dani men. They could have as many wives as they could afford. What they could afford was dependent on the number of pigs they owned. Pigs were the main commodity used in bartering for wives. We learned the usual number required was three or four pigs to arrange for a bride payment. Polygamy was one sided. Men could have as many wives as they could afford, but women could have only one husband.

Although marriages were arranged when the girls were beginning puberty it might be two or more years before the marriage were consummated. The girl would continue to live with her family until certain obligations were met by the man. When that period of time elapsed, the girl would be given two marriage gifts. She would be given a newly sharpened stick for gardening and a new skirt which symbolized her maturity in adulthood. This skirt was made of strings created from hand-rolled bark that wrapped around her lower torso, just above the pubic area. She would not live in her husband's honai, but rather in a separate honai reserved for females. If her husband already had other wives, she would move into the honai with those wives.

Sexual relations would then commence until the wife became pregnant. Once the wife became pregnant, the husband and wife would cease having sexual relations. This abstinence of sex between husband and wife would continue for a period of time ranging from two to six years. Once the baby was born, it was the wife's responsibility to breast feed the child until they were five or six years old.

Families were small, usually one to two children. By the time the wife was 18-20 years of age, and had borne one or two children, she was done with child bearing. Mortality rate of children was high. Almost fifty per cent of children died before their tenth birthday. There were very few diseases in the valley, but living conditions were harsh. The strong would survive, the weak would perish. It was all part of the circle of life for the Dani.

The Dani had another ingenious way of keeping the population to a manageable level. When a woman was at the end of child bearing, she would drink the sap from a certain tree that grew in the valley. This sap would cause the woman to slip into early menopause making her incapable of becoming pregnant in the future. There were some practical reasons for this. The valley was only 80 kilometers long and twenty some kilometers wide. It could not support a large population of people. There simply would not be enough resources in land and food to feed a growing population.

Women were expected to look after the children, grow crops in the gardens, and look after the pigs. Pigs were the most valuable commodity that a man had and it was expected that they would be watched closely. They were allowed to roam free during the daytime. When evening came, they were collected and brought into the confines of the village where they would be kept in the long house that served as both the cooking area and the nighttime pens for the pigs. Pigs were so valued that they were sometimes stolen by other tribesmen. If that happened, it would be the fault of the women and the children for not watching the pigs as closely as they should have.

We were told not to venture into the longhouse of a village. Some villages had more than one long house, depending on how many wives the village men and the village chief had. It was not a social taboo to enter a longhouse. The reason for not entering the longhouse is that every longhouse was infested with lice. That is all the advice we needed to give the longhouses a wide berth.

We would often see the women sitting outside their longhouses going through each other's hair looking for lice and nits.

The Dani women and their husbands could get, what we in the west would call a divorce, although that was very uncommon. Wives would sometimes leave their husbands compound and return to their own villages to live separately from their husbands for extended periods of time.

A Dani wife had one other duty in regard to the pigs. If the mother sow was off someplace foraging for food, the Dani women would suckle the little piglets. Such was the status of pigs in the Dani culture. The right breast of a woman was for her children, the left breast was for the piglets. The left breast would often become elongated as compared to the right breast. I don't recall seeing the piglets suckle at a human breast, but we saw plenty of examples of the elongated left breast.

Like I mentioned, we were there to observe and learn, not to judge. Although this duty of breast feeding the piglets would be completely unacceptable in a western culture, it was deeply ingrained in the Dani culture.

The women would go to the gardens early in the mornings and work until near sundown. There was no real defined meal time. The Dani ate when they were hungry. They would eat a certain variety of sweet potato in the morning and a different variety in the evening. The sweet potatoes were huge, much larger than the types we would see in grocery stores in the United States.

Since there were several gardens at different stages of development going on at the same time, there was plenty of work to be done. The only tool at the disposal of the women was the sharpened stick. With this sharpened stick, they cultivated the gardens, and dug up the sweet potatoes when they were done growing. They grew cucumbers, tobacco, greens, ginger, taro, yams and carrots.

Bananas were the only crop grown within the village.

The Dani women did this back bending labor day after day, planting, irrigating when necessary, hoeing, and cultivating.

They grew into an acceptance of their life's upcoming work at a young age. Little girls played at being an adult. They would have tiny gardens in which they planted seeds. Little boys practiced war games. Each sex came to accept their roles at an early age. A man's job was to create. A woman's job was to listen, follow, and produce.

I asked one of our Dani interpreters one day if the women ever complained about the unequal distribution of work.

Hella, the interpreter, looked at me and smiled. "No," he said, "a woman would never do that. They simply do whatever their husbands tell them to do."

The chief of the first village we visited had 18 wives. We found out that another village chief had 23 wives.

I guess both chiefs had a lot of pigs.

Killian, chief of Wyagoba village had a different problem. Killian quickly became our favorite chief. We spent more time with him than any other chief, even Wali. Killian simply had a presence about him. He was strong of build, had obvious leadership qualities, smiled broadly, and it was obvious that his villagers respected him.

We found out Killian's problem is that he had only one wife. That alone would have set Killian apart from other chiefs in the valley. Killian's problem was that he had been married for some years and he and his wife still had no children. The chief of a village was expected to have a male heir to follow him as the next village chief.

Willem said that this was becoming a topic of conversation among the villagers. If Killian's wife did not soon produce a child, preferably a male child, villagers would force Killian to take another wife to produce that heir.

If you thought the idea of breast feeding the piglets was about the most disgusting thing you ever heard of, then perhaps you do not want to hear of the Dani practice of "Ikipalin."

Ikipalin means finger cutting. Fingers symbolize harmony, unity, and force within an individual or a family. The Dani believe that by cutting off a finger up to the first digit can alleviate any misfortune in a family due to a death of one of its members.

All female family members go through Ikipalin once a family member dies. The finger cutting is voluntary, but we were assured that all females feel the responsibility to cut off part of a finger. We saw many old women with all of their fingers cut off up to the first digit, except for the thumb.

The finger is tied off, cutting off most or all of the circulation to the finger which is to be cut. This cutting off of circulation lasts about thirty minutes. At the end of the thirty minute time period, there is little or no feeling in the finger. The finger may already be dead. The finger is severed by use of a stone axe, sharpened bamboo knives, or, in rare cases, it may even be chewed off. The severed finger is then cauterized with fire to prevent infection. The cauterization also causes a thick callus to form over the severed finger.

The Dani cremate their dead. In a separate ceremony, the severed portion of the finger is also burned and the ashes kept and stored by the family.

The practice of Ikipalin had been outlawed sometime before we arrived in 1980. The strange thing was we saw several young girls with their hands wrapped in grass. The grass was held in place with a vine that was wrapped around the hand.

I asked Willem about this and he kept repeating that the practice was outlawed and it could not be done any longer. After I had seen several young girls, perhaps 14 or 15 years old, with their hands wrapped in such a fashion I again asked Willem what was going on. After some badgering, Willem finally admitted that the practice still existed. The girls would be taken into the jungle, away from prying eyes to do the amputation. Willem did admit that even though the finger was numbed, the women still cried when their finger was amputated.

The Indonesian officials must have known what was going on, but resisted doing anything about it. Asia is strange that way. Sometimes there are laws that are strictly observed and sometimes there are laws that exist, but are not always enforced. It is a strange concept for westerners to understand.

You peel back the onion only to find yet another layer of the onion.

In addition to cutting off a digit of their finger when a relative died, women still had one more duty to perform in the death ritual. They would cover their entire body with mud. The mud would become caked on when it dried. There would be a mourning period of three months and then in a ceremony the woman would be bathed, the mud washed off, and the body cleansed to end the period of mourning.

The incongruity in the disparity of work and the sacrifices for death rituals the women were required to do compared to the men was stark and a bit hard to wrap our brains around. That polygamy was a one-way street, with men having as many wives as they could afford based on the number of pigs they owned, was also a bit mind boggling.

Yacoom, a Dani with a real sense of humor, would often ask my wife is she was happily married. We were out walking one day and had stopped for a break. Tea, which was our drink of choice, was mixed with Tang and we sat on the ground, took a break, and tried to hydrate.

Yacoom picked up a stray pig that had wondered by. He began stroking the pig as he asked me if I might be interested in possibly bartering my wife away for some of these fine pigs. He was kidding, of course, but we both got a kick out of the bantering. He offered three pigs and I pretended to be insulted with such a low offer.

My wife, I said, was worth more than three pigs.

Negotiations stalled, the tea mixed with Tang was all gone and we prepared to continue our walk. Yacoom kept stroking the pig, when all of a sudden he saw a large bug that looked something like a smooth skinned caterpillar on the back of the pig. He picked up the bug, and without a moment's hesitation, popped it in his mouth. I heard one crunch and it was gone.

The pig was released without being turned over to a new owner.

I still had my wife.

Thanks to the pig, Yacoom had an unexpected bit of protein added to his diet. In a valley where protein was in very short supply except on those occasions when a pig was slaughtered for a village ceremony, every bit of protein was welcome, even if it did come from a bug.

We got up, stretched, and started to walk to the next village. The rest had provided us with one more story to tell about eating bugs for protein. Nothing much about Dani life surprised us anymore.

We walked on.

The journey continued.

Life was good.

XEROX
COPY SERVICE

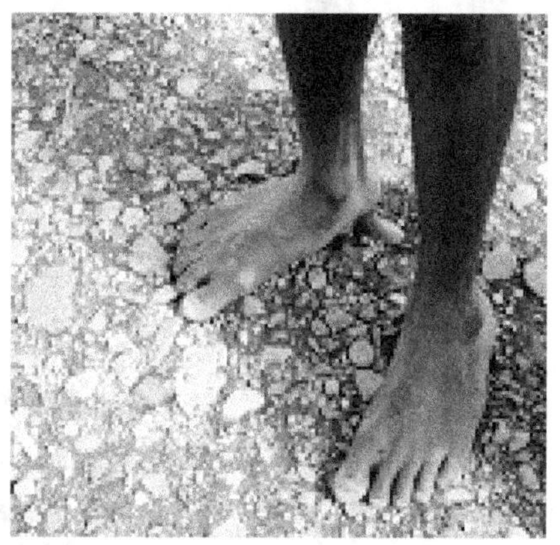

14

GATHERING SALT

We spent Christmas Eve in Killian's honai. Wali was with us as were several other Dani tribesmen. We talked, asked questions and had questions asked of us. It was obvious in the questions they ask that the Dani are intelligent people. If they had been born elsewhere, outside the confines of the small valley where they were raised, would they have been doctors, lawyers, construction workers, or possibly, just like us, teachers?

We had brought framed photos of Killian and Wali from teacher friends who had visited a year prior to our arrival. The presents were wrapped in tissue paper and we had our cameras out to see the reaction of each chief as they removed the wrapping of their photo. We had brought in flashlights so we would have more than just the fire in the middle of the honai for light.   We wanted to be able to see the facial expressions when the two chiefs saw a photo of themselves.

We watched as each chief unwrapped the tissue holding his photo, our cameras at the ready, our anticipation growing, each of us wanting to see their reaction as they viewed the first photo ever taken of them.

What happened next was another of the many amazing moments of an already amazing trip.   Each chief peered at their photo, their image captured on film . . . AND . . . they did not recognize themselves in the photo.   They both ended up looking at the photo of the other chief, pointing their finger at that photo simultaneously.   Killian recognized the photo of Wali, just as Wali was recognizing the photo of Killian.   Neither of them recognized the photo of themselves because they had never, in their lifetime, seen their own reflection.   The rivers in the valley are always a muddy brown and they had never seen a mirror, so, of course, they had never seen any image of themselves.

They both broke into infectious smiles and the ensuing photo that Kathy Wasosky took, two Dani chiefs pointing fingers at each other, turned out to be one of the best photos of the trip.

We felt bad that we had not packed the small mirrors that we had been advised to bring along with us. We feared they would be broken in transit so we left them behind. There was nothing we could do about that now. We still had one unforgettable photo, each chief recognizing the other, but not their own image.

We went to bed that night feeling we already had our Christmas present with the reaction we had seen on the chiefs' faces. The night turned cold and I had to get up, put on long pants, socks, and a jacket to get a few fitful hours of rest, again pulling the makeshift sleeping sack up around me, periodically coming up for air to fight claustrophobia. Once I did that, I would be immediately bombarded by mosquitoes.

We woke up at 6:30 in the morning, wished each other a Merry Christmas, and made our way out of the chief's honai. The Dani were already up, arms thrown across their chests, trying to preserve warmth in the early morning chill.

We had brought a small tape player with us on the trip and one of our group of six put in a Christmas tape. We didn't even try to explain the significance of the Christmas carol that was playing to the Dani tribesmen.

Our Christmas breakfast consisted of roasted bananas supplied by the Dani women. One of the women had cut down a large bunch of bananas, there was a fire already burning, and the whole stalk of bananas lay sizzling on a bed of coals. The bananas were turned several times, taken off the flames, and we all had a healthy meal of roasted bananas. It was one of the better breakfasts we would have during our stay in the valley.

Soon after the warm breakfast of bananas, tea, and snacks, we were off once again. We basked in the early morning sun, the valley growing brighter and warmer with each passing moment, all thoughts of the fitful night's sleep fighting cold and mosquitoes behind us. We were off on what we were sure would be an eventful day. We would walk on paths for four hours until we reached a new village, a new adventure, a village where we would again trade for some more souvenirs.

We continued to see women working in their fields, digging sweet potatoes and hoeing. For lunch we had a sweet potato. My potato was so big I couldn't finish all of it. Besides, I was already getting tired of sweet potatoes.

We arrived in a new village and were once again greeted warmly by the villagers. The Dani were just being introduced to missionaries and the belief in Christianity. Most Dani were still animists, believing that the soul of a person resided in all living matter. They believed in the existence of spirits and demons. They believed in ghosts and ancestor worship.

Just as we were leaving the village we saw a pile of rocks stacked on top of each other. In addition to the rocks, there were also bits of wood stacked in with the rocks. The whole thing looked out of place to us so we asked Willem what the pile of rocks and wood represented. He told us it was a religious alter, that the Dani believed in an afterlife, and that they prayed to this alter.

We had only spent a short period of time in the village, trading for some more souvenirs, before we were told it was time to leave. When we asked where we were going, we were told we were going to see how salt was gathered by the Dani villages.

Everyone needs salt in their diet, but where were the Dani going to get salt in a valley far from the sea? We asked Willem this question and he replied that there were only two places in the entire valley where the different Dani tribes could get salt, and we were very near one of those places. We walked a ways on level ground but then started a gradual ascent up through the jungle canopy. The rocks we were climbing over became more and more slippery. We had to be careful to avoid falling. The rocks had been worn bare from generations of Dani climbing to the spot where the salt was to be found. Not wanting to fall on the rocks, we moved more slowly until we finally arrived at a small pool of stagnant looking water. The water wasn't deep and its surface was covered with scum.

The pool itself was no more than a few meters long and about the same in width. In the middle of the stagnant pool, was a Dani woman and what looked like a teenage girl who may have been her daughter. They each had noken on their heads and they were bent over soaking something in the water.

The something they were soaking in the water turned out to be a banana plant. They would peel off a layer from the banana plant, repeatedly plunge the layer of the plant into the water, soaking it in the salt brine. They would stop every so often and chew the layers of banana plant until it became a pulpy blob. They would then return to soaking the chewed pulp back in the water.

Willem explained that salt seeped out of the ground and into this particular rock formation. No one, including Willem, seemed to understand why this phenomenon occurred, but this pool of salty brine water had been in this location longer than anyone could remember.

The two women would stay in the pool of water, whose depth seemed to go just past the women's knees, until all of the banana plant would be stripped apart, soaked, chewed, dunked back into the water numerous times until they were satisfied that enough salt had permeated the plant. The soaking takes about two hours before they start back down the mountain and back to their village.

When this work was finally done, the banana plant, now a pulpy mess would be carried down to the village where the banana plant would be dried, burned and gathered up to mix with some other substance to make a kind of rock salt. The Dani would eat the rock salt in order to get the necessary salt in their diet.

This is the way all the Dani tribes got their salt and it had been going on this way for untold generations, each tribe sending women up to strip banana plants, soak them in the briny water, chew the fibers, and soak them again. It is always amazing the way civilizations adapt to the geography they live in. What they wear, what their houses are like, what they eat is dependent on what they can grow or hunt. All of those factors are dependent on the geography they live in.

There was one funny incident that happened as we were watching the two women go about gathering salt that remains a vivid part of my memory of that day. We had brought along several cases of 7-Up for this trip. We limited ourselves to one can per day and that one can of 7-Up became our small daily luxury. I was getting very tired of tea and had starting mixing Tang with the tea to give it a slightly different flavor. Even this drink was getting tiresome, so I decided I was going to have my daily can of 7-Up as I watched the women work. I was feeling dehydrated and the thought of the 7-Up, even a warm 7-Up, became overpowering. I popped the tab on the can and quickly downed the drink.

I wasn't thinking anything of it, just holding the empty can in my hand. Five or six Dani men had accompanied us up the mountain. They always seemed in the mood to go on any outing that was taking place, and we were now used to an entourage of Dani men tagging along. One of these men sidled up close to me and indicated the empty can by pointing his finger. It took me a few seconds to figure out that he would appreciate it if I gave him the empty can. I never gave it another thought and quickly handed him the empty soda can. He also indicated that he wanted the pull tab which I happily passed over as well. He took the can, dipped it into the scummy, briny water, filled the can to the top, and slowly started sipping the salty brine. How their intestinal system ever adjusted to this disgusting looking water is a mystery. If we would have tried to drink the water, (not that any of us would have been brave enough to try it) we would expect to be on our death bed within minutes.

We all thought this was pretty humorous to see a Dani tribesman using a soda can to drink salt water. I looked away for a few minutes, continuing to watch the two women do their thing, alternating dunking and chewing the banana plant. When I looked back, I saw why the Dani man wanted both the empty soda can and the pop top tab. He had his ears pierced and he had somehow gotten the pull tab inserted in his ear lobe. He now had a perfectly fine looking earring. He looked proud as punch with what he had just accomplished.

It has been nearly four decades since I saw the Dani tribesman drinking salt water from a 7-Up can, but I still think of that man on occasion. The Dani tribes do not produce pottery. They lap up water with their hands from a puddle or stream until they have had their fill. Here was a man who now had a vessel for carrying and drinking water. What was junk to me, trash I had to dispose of, was a treasure to him. He came away from a short journey up a mountain with something he could use. He also came away with a new earring.

Every once in a while as I pick up my salt shaker preparing to salt my food, I think back on that day, climbing a mountain path worn smooth by generations on a trip to gather salt.

I think of the man who simply wanted an empty soda can and a pull tab. I can still see the man slowly sipping salt water from a brackish pool. It is just as clear to me today as it was all those years ago.

When I picture him in my mind's eye, I realize that the day on the mountain, gathering salt, was a great day for both of us.

15

PIG ROAST

We came down from the mountain where the salt was being harvested and walked back to Killian's village. We never saw the two women who had been gathering salt once we left the mountain. Perhaps they were from another village and had to carry their cargo of banana pulp soaked in salt brine even further than we had walked. Walking was the only way for the Dani to get from one place to another so distance, like time, was irrelevant. If you had to travel, you had to walk, so what difference did it make how far something was from your home village. You walked, and it took whatever time it took to get there and get back.

After we got back to Killian's village we had a lunch of rice and then started to walk to yet another village where we once again traded for head nets covered in feathers, wild boars tusks, and bows and arrows. I had pretty much done all of the bartering I wanted to do. I had bows, arrows, a long spear with a cassowary birds toe as the point of the spear, some head nets covered in feathers, a noken, a bone knife made from what I think is the femur of a cassowary bird, and a stone axe. I had seen the Dani use the stone axe to cut down medium sized trees. The stone, about the size and shape of an axe, was wedged between an L-shaped branch cut from a small tree. Wooden wedges were inserted around the stone which prevented the stone from becoming dislodged. The stone had not been sharpened in any manner. It had been tapered naturally, tumbling down a river until it was finally deposited in the stream bed. The rock remained there until a Dani found it, pulled it from the river bank, and fixed it into an axe handle.

It took about an hour to walk to Wali's village after we were done trading for more items. Wali's village was called Opaghima and it turned out to be the best organized village we were to see during our time in the Baliem Valley. It was even organized better than Killian's village.

All of this was due, I suspect, to Wali. He wasn't just an older version of Killian; he had also fought in more raids and wars than Killian. When you were in the presence of these two chiefs, there was little doubt they were men of high standing. The reverence in which they were held by villagers was impossible not to notice. They were bright, intelligent men; well organized and brave. Both men commanded respect from everyone in their village. It was obvious to all of us that they genuinely liked each other. Their embraces were long and gentle, their voices low and welcoming.

The Dani have a number of celebrations throughout the year and each of these celebrations requires pigs to be slaughtered and roasted. A man with a herd of twenty pigs was considered rich.   The pig herd had to keep growing in order to have enough pigs on hand for upcoming celebrations or arranging for a new wife.

Wali made the pronouncement that his village would have a pig roast to celebrate our arrival in the valley. Before we left on the trip, Sjam told us to expect a pig roast at some point in our stay with the Dani, but she warned us not to eat any of the meat. Since none of us was enamored with the prospect of getting a tape worm or some other disease from eating pork we all declined the offer to eat the pig meat.

A small pig was brought out, with the emphasis placed on small. Wali was apologetic about the size of the pig. We were a day behind our carefully laid out itinerary on arriving at Wali's village due to losing the first flight from Jakarta. Wali said he had a much larger pig the previous day, but when we did not arrive as planned he let the pig go. This little pig was so small that there wouldn't have been much meat to go around anyway, so none of the Dani men seemed the least upset that we were not going to indulge in eating any of the pork.

Wali brought out a bow and arrow and the doomed little pig was held up by two Dani tribesmen. The pig was stretched out, two Dani men holding the pig aloft, pulling the squealing pig by gripping the front and hind legs. Wali stood about ten feet away with his bow and arrow, then, perhaps thinking better of it, moved in closer to six feet away. It was pretty obvious that Wali, a warrior who had fought many battles that involved life and death, did not want to embarrass himself by missing the pig.

His aim was true, the arrow piercing the little pig near the rib cage. Copious amounts of blood started to flow from the pig.   The little pig squealed as loudly as it could before the Dani holders put the little pig on the ground. The pig took off on a death run, squealing with each stride. The pig circled part of the courtyard before his legs gave out under him and he dropped over, dead.

Wali smiled; perhaps, relieved he had not missed with his arrow and embarrassed himself.

Killian laughed.

We applauded.

The little pig was taken over to a fire and his hair was burned off until his skin started to crack. A small piece of bamboo was sharpened with an axe. This would serve as a knife. Once sharpened, the bamboo knife was surprisingly sharp. The ears and tail were cut off the pig and then the pig was gutted and split in two.

A large fire had been started in the courtyard of the village. Large stones, most were a bit smaller than a volleyball, were heating up in the fire. About eight or ten village women were tending the fire. Some of these women were covered with mud, signifying they were in their three month mourning period for a deceased relative. They each had poles longer than their bodies. The ends of the poles had been split four ways. This split allowed the women to push the hot rocks up into the split area of the pole. The rocks were then carried to a pit that was in the center of the courtyard.

The pit was about three feet deep. If you held your arms out and made a circle with them, you would still be short of having the circumference of the pit. Women began putting grass in the bottom of the pit. Once that task was completed, rocks were added to the pit. The grass was green so nothing started on fire. More grass was added to the sides of the pit and on top of the rocks. Cabbages, greens, and sweet potatoes were added on top of the grass. More grass followed, then another layer of sweet potatoes. The pit, with grass, potatoes, cabbages, and greens was now higher than the depth of the pit. The pig was then placed near top of the pit. More grass was piled on until the entire structure was perhaps three feet above ground level.

The grass that was above ground level was held together by vines that were wrapped around the entire structure. Having done this ceremony many times before as dictated by custom, the whole process was all very efficient, each woman knowing her task, working as a team, chattering away with each other as they worked. They seemed to be having as much fun preparing the pit as we were in watching them work in such a synchronized fashion.

The pit started to do its job. Smoke rose through the grass from the heated rocks below and the aroma of roasting potatoes, vegetables, and pork filled the village courtyard.

We again sat on flat boards provided for our comfort, taking photos as the process unfolded before us, swatted flies that insisted we were their landing strip, and waited for the dinner ingredients to be cooked. It took about two hours before the women announced that dinner was ready. The women detached the vines and pulled apart the grass, as steam continued to rise from the pit. We had evidence that the heated stones had done their job by the steaming sweet potatoes pulled from the pit.

I started to eat my sweet potato but it was so large that I only finished a third of it before I gave the rest to a small boy who happily gobbled it down.

Wali, Killian, and some of the tribesmen ate the pig. The women, we were told, got none of the meat because the pig was too little.

In the two hours we waited for the pig to finish cooking, we learned a few things about Wali's village. The long house where the regular cooking was to be done had two fire pits. Wali had ten wives, so he needed a larger long house to accommodate his wives and pigs.

Wali's honai was also different than any other we saw in the valley. His honai had two stories instead of the usual one story.

It was really a house within a house. The outside frame of the house was the same as any honai. Once you stepped inside the honai there was a gap of about three feet which lead to the inner house. This three foot gap served as an insulation barrier.

Darkness had fallen and we were invited into Wali's honai. We only had a sweet potato for dinner so our meal of rice, vegetables, soup and tea was brought into the honai. This same meal was served every day and we became just as tired of this meal as we did with eating sweet potatoes. We weren't in the valley for any culinary experience so we sat on mats spread on the floor and ate without complaint. Fresh grass covered the floor as it did in each honai.

Wali had invited quite a few men into his honai and they waited patiently as we finished our meal. They were content to smoke their cigarettes and talk among themselves until we were ready to join in the conversation.

We spent most of the rest of the evening asking questions. The Dani men lazed about, some sitting, others lying in a prone position, all smoking. They chatted among themselves, always patient, answering our questions and asking questions of us. Except for the smoke from the pit fire and the Dani smoking cigarettes, it was all very relaxing. It was like talking to your neighbor over a backyard fence.

It was a nice way to unwind after our busy day of climbing a mountain to gather salt.

16

THE TAPE RECORDER
AND THE AMULET

We were in Wali's honai again. There were a number of village elders who had joined us for another evening of conversation, and of course, smoking. We had brought in more cigarettes for them to smoke. The amount of cigarettes we had packed for the trip was proving woefully inadequate. We did bring along a few cigars, figuring that a cigar was something none of them had probably ever tried before. A cigar would be lit and handed out to an elder tribesman. He would take one or two puffs and then pass it on to the next Dani.

We were learning that sharing seemed to be an integral part

of the Dani society. The cigars were passed from one to another allowing each Dani an opportunity to try these 'big cigarettes.' Before long the hut was filling with smoke from the fire pit, the cigars, and the cigarettes the men were smoking incessantly. None of us smoked, so it wasn't always pleasant being in closed quarters where smoking was second nature to both men and women. The Dani elders, on the other hand, were completely at ease, laughing, smoking, and telling stories. They were acting no different than anyone else in the world that might be having a beer with friends after work or talking about the last soccer match they had watched on television.

We sat around the honai, smoke rising, grass the only padding for our seats. We started to ask questions and fell into the elongated version of translations that were required before our questions could be answered. Our questions would be relayed to Willem, then on to Hella, a Dani tribesman who had been taught Bahasa Indonesian by missionaries. Hella would translate the question into the Dani dialect. Once the Dani understood our question, they would converse among themselves until they settled on an appropriate response.

They would speak with Hella and the chain of languages would reverse until we got our question answered in English by Willem. Although this process took time, the Dani, never ones to be concerned with the western concept of time, were extremely patient in answering all of our questions. Some things are always lost when you are doing translations in multiple languages, but we did the best we could, everyone laughed a lot, and a real sense of camaraderie was felt by all.

We asked about the finger cutting, which was now technically illegal, but still being practiced. The Dani men admitted that even though the finger was tied off and numbed for some time before the ceremony took place, the women still cried when their finger was severed.

It seemed so strange to us that women could seem happy when life was so harsh for them. Willem said women basically had no rights. If you are bought for pigs, I guess you accept the fact that you will obey all rules established by the men who trade for you. They accepted their role in the village as one who worked in the fields, took care of children, cooked the meals, and didn't ask questions of their status. Their simple pleasures were smoking, cooking together in the long houses with other women, and socializing. In the time we were in the valley, I never spoke to a woman, nor did I have the opportunity to speak to one of them. They left the impression of being shy, mostly staying in the background, and either had no interest in interacting with us or had been instructed not to speak with us.

Killian and Wali once again brought up the possibility of flying on an airplane to Jayapura so they could see a modern city. We didn't have the heart to tell the two chiefs that Jayapura was far from a modern city. We had heard this story just a few days before but Willem informed us the two chiefs ask him about their dream to fly on a plane every time he sees them. They keep saying it is their wish to make such a trip and they even dream about it when they sleep.

Willem informed them once again that they would have to bathe and wear clothes when they went to Jayapura. Both of the chiefs said that they had no problem taking a bath and wearing clothes although they had never worn clothes before and it was questionable how many times they had ever taken a bath. Their final answer concerning wearing clothes was most telling of their thinking. They said not only would they wear clothes but that they would be ashamed if they did not wear clothes. They knew they were primitive. They had been told this by missionaries and Indonesian officials as well. They just wanted to fit in when they went to Jayapura like everyone else.

They didn't want to stand out and be different. They didn't want to be stared at.

I couldn't help thinking that the Dani were not that much different than the rest of us. Don't we all just want to blend in?

We eventually ran out of questions to ask. Someone suggested that the tables should be turned and the Dani should ask us questions. They asked if we had only come to take photos, since it seemed that is what we were doing most of the time. They asked a few questions about the outside world, but I'm not sure they really understood what the outside world was like. To them, we were the outside world. We looked different, wore different clothes, ate different food, and certainly had different tools. How could we explain subway systems, zoos, sky scrapers, elections, traffic jams, or nuclear weapons?

Pam had brought a tape recorder along on the trip. When questions started to wane she took it out so we could show the Dani how we could record our voices and the machine would play back what we had just said. The Dani became so excited about this new piece of equipment they could hardly contain themselves.

They figured out that the tape recorder wasn't a camera because it didn't flash when it was turned on, but they had never seen anything like it before. We had Hella ask the tribesmen if they wanted to speak into the tape recorder and have their words played back for them. There was universal agreement that this sounded like a grand idea. They got these huge smiles on their faces which was all the answer we needed. We turned on the recorder and one of the Dani would give a short speech. We would stop the recording, rewind the tape, and then hit the play button. The Dani listened, spellbound, as they heard their recorded voices for the first time. They would start to listen to the recording and then laughter would break out from everyone in the honai. The Dani laughed because they recognized their voices on a machine which to them was a miracle, something beyond plausibility.

We laughed because of the reactions of the Dani. Their mouths were agape, shock showing in their expressions, unable to fully grasp exactly what was happening. Whether they understood what was happening with the machine or not, one thing was clear, the Dani wanted each man to have the opportunity to have his voice recorded. The recorder got passed from one man to the next. Sometimes only one person spoke, sometimes several spoke, many times all of them chimed in. They wanted the recorder rewound time after time so they could hear the recording over and over again. The Dani were having a great time. This was a first for them. We, on the other hand, soon tired of hearing the same recordings played over, and over, and over again.

We tried politely to move on to something else but the Dani wanted none of that. They were hearing their recorded voices for the first time and they never seemed to get tired of listening to themselves on the tape player. I think they could have spent the rest of the night listening to their voices. They seemed like children, not the fierce warriors with boar's tusks in their nostrils that had gone into battle over land, pigs, and the ritual warfare that was so much a part of their culture.

I don't know if it was the relaxed atmosphere in the honai that night, if it was the recording that seemed to please the Dani so much, or if it was something altogether different that set off what happened next.

Wali's brother got up to give a speech. The speech was long and rambling, and of course we didn't understand a word of it.

He was holding something in his hand, something small and unattractive. There was a string attached to the object and Wali's brother was obviously giving a speech about this object because all of the Dani eyes were now laser focused on him. Just a few minutes before laughter dominated the honai. Now all of that had changed. There was electricity in the air; something in the whole atmosphere of the honai had changed once the speech started. We sat there in silence, knowing something was different, yet we weren't sure exactly what was transpiring.

Wali's brother walked towards us and was trying to give us the object in his hand. We asked Willem to interpret, and Willem, in turn, asked Hella to translate. What Wali's brother held in his hand was a village amulet, a talisman, a charm. It was an object worn on the body that the Dani believed held great power. It was a charm which the Dani believed helped to protect the village; it promoted the growth of crops and kept the village safe. He was giving us something that had belonged in the village for a long period of time. He placed the amulet over Gene Wasosky's head and that is when all hell broke loose.

Each of the Dani tribesmen seemed to be speaking at the same time. If you believed their body language, not all of the tribesmen were happy with giving away such a powerful gift. All six of us became quite nervous. The tribesmen seemed to be arguing with each other. Voices were raised. We still didn't know exactly what was going on, we just knew it wasn't good.

The amulet had already been presented to Gene. Hella, the translator, said that many of the village elders did not want to see the amulet go far away from the valley. They feared, he said, that the power the amulet would be diminished, its power lost to the village.

We agreed almost immediately that we wanted to give the amulet back, but didn't know how to do that. The Dani continued their debate well into the night. We went to bed, although I am not sure any of us slept very well. Gene kept the amulet with him since we weren't going anyplace other than where we were right now, in Wali's honai.

The mosquitoes were bigger and hungrier than in Killian's village. With the unsettling event surrounding the amulet and the veracity of the mosquito attacks, it was impossible to sleep. I kept waking up after just a few minutes of sleep, checking my watch, disappointed that we were still hours from morning light. I finally fell asleep around four when the night had turned cold. The mosquitoes had departed, no doubt engorged on our blood. I figured in the last four days I had not had more than 15 hours sleep in total.

We awoke the next morning with the issue of the amulet still unsettled. It became apparent to us that we must find a way to give the amulet back to the village. Gene came to the rescue. He gave a nice little speech, translated by Hella, expressing our pleasure in giving us such a valuable object but we could not possibly accept such a powerful gift. The amulet belonged in the village and in the village it must stay.

The Dani were gracious in accepting the return of an item that was very important to them. All of us saved face, the Dani got their powerful talisman back and we could once again relax. The world of the Dani was again in alignment.

Looking back on that evening, I can't help but think of the old world of the Dani, little changed in millennia, and the new world that we represented that had intersected the previous evening in the honai. The new was represented by the tape recorder which the Dani loved. Having given the Dani the magic of hearing their own voices recorded on a machine, brought them a little closer to the modern world. Giving us the amulet was a gift from an ancient culture; informing us of a belief that an amulet had more power over a village than human reason.

Neither gesture worked well. The Dani did not deserve to

be thrown into the modern world at breakneck speed, and we did not belong in their world. The issue was settled, but it was a harbinger of problems to come. The Dani tribes wanted very much to retain their ancestral culture, but were being pulled into a modern world they were not adequately prepared to join.

We were learning things from the Dani tribe each day, but we had certain advantages they did not possess. We had been granted an education. We knew of the modern world and how quickly things could change. We knew time was running out on the Dani tribes, their culture and their traditions. We didn't know how things would end, but we feared it would not end well for a tribe of people that we had come to like and respect.

17

THE OLD WOMAN WITH THE WOUNDS

After we had given back the amulet we were all able to relax. We had our usual breakfast of rice, toast, and tea.

By 8 a.m. we had finished breakfast. We said our "laoaks and naraks" to Wali and his tribe's people and off we went on another long walk. Killian was going to be with us for the whole day. There were so many characteristics that made Killian stand out to us more than any other Dani we were to meet on our trip. He was tall, erect, and his smile was electric. He had an air about him that just said, "leader." Another characteristic about Killian was that he was very helpful. He had a great willingness to work. He carried part of our luggage as we set off on another day of long marches. He was always there to help us cross ditches and streams. This was no small feat because there had been a heavy rain the previous night. Everything was wet and slippery. All of us got quite wet and muddy. Each of us fell at least once due to the wet conditions.

We were headed for the village Pabuma. The Chief of Pabuma was a man named Obaharok. He was one of the chiefs that we had promised to deliver a shovel head to. This was the last shovel we had to deliver and we were looking forward to getting rid of it and lightening our load.

We arrived in the village of Pabuma but Obaharok was not there. A man in a neighboring village had died and Obaharok was with the family of the deceased. The deceased was to be cremated that afternoon so we surmised we would not see Obaharok.

We had been told that Pabuma was one of the nicest villages in the valley but this turned out not to be true. Pabuma turned out to be the dirtiest village we had visited. There were flies everywhere and we spent the entire time in the village swatting away those pesky flies. The flies, undeterred, would simple circle and come back to land on you again.

I saw an old woman come out of a hut and head for some standing water to wash. The woman turned out to be the oldest wife of Obaharok.

Willem had been dressing a toe of one of the Dani porters who was traveling with us. He had come to help with crossing ditches. In some places, downed trees that were cut and placed over ditches or ravines were our only way of crossing to the other side. Since the Dani do not own shoes, they naturally go barefoot everywhere. The stones on the paths were sharp; it had been a wet and very sloppy day in which we would step in the mud and sink up to mid-calf.

One of the villagers told Willem that the old lady we had seen, who was indeed Obaharok's oldest wife, was ill. The Dani did not say what was wrong with her, just that she was not well and would we take a look at her.

We had packed a small med kit with some very basic supplies. We had tape, band-aids, an ankle wrap in case of a sprained foot, some antibiotic ointment, Imodium, sun screen, aspirin, and a few other items that might get us through a minor injury. At that time, we probably had taken malarial prophylactics. But, we had not packed anything in case we had a serious injury. If something catastrophic had gone wrong with us, we would have had to be carried back to Wamena and wait for the next plane to arrive. Since planes could only arrive during clear weather, we were at the mercy of the weather and our own carelessness when it came to injury or disease.

We were all young, so we had taken the chance that nothing would go wrong; the health gods would look upon us with favor and allow us to escape without some dreadful disease like dengue fever or malaria and we eventually all could fly out of Wamena in good health.

We went to where the old woman was sitting, not far from a puddle of brown water she had used to wash herself. The first thing we noticed was that the woman was indeed very old. It wasn't just her wrinkled skin or the thin skeletal frame. All of her fingers on both hands were missing up to the first digit. She had sacrificed much for those family members who had died before her.

She wore only the skirt of a married woman. Her only other adornment was a filthy cloth thrown over part of her back. She said not a word as she threw back the cloth. She had a hideous wound on her back that had liquid oozing out of it. The open sore was covered with pus and she had yet another open sore on her wrist.

Flies were landing on her back. We would try and swat them away but they would circle and immediately land on the wound.

We heated some warm water and used some clean cloth to wash the dirt and grime out of the wound. The old woman never flinched, and her face remained placid although she must have been in intense pain. We did not have any penicillin with us because even we could not get penicillin for our journey without a prescription. We had thought enough ahead to get some sulfa powder and that was the only thing we had that could possibly fight infection. We sprinkled the sulfa powder over the wound as best we could. We took off the filthy rag she had placed over the wound and Willem told the Dani man who had asked us to look at Obaharok's wife, to not let the old woman put the filthy rag on her back again. She had to let the air help heal the wound, had to keep the wound washed with warm water to keep it clean, and she had to try to keep the flies away from the wound. All this information we passed on to the tribesman.

We had some antibiotic tablets with us which we made her take. That was all any of us could do. Willem left some of the tablets with a villager as we walked out of the village. None of us wanted to stay any longer because of the flies. We would never know what had happened to the woman or what had caused her injuries. Had she fallen in a ditch, hitting a rock? Had she fallen while crossing one of the trees that had been downed to cross a ravine?

We also would never know if she would live or die. It was one of those moments when you realize how fragile life can be. You learn quickly that in the Baliem Valley you can live or die with the slip of a foot, an infection, or an illness. Death is a part of life here and there is no one to help you if something goes wrong. You are on your own. You live. You die. You get better or you get worse.

You are mourned if you die, a female family member will

sacrifice a finger for your journey to the afterworld. No matter what, life goes on.

Obaharok never did show up, so after an hour we left the village, grateful to be away from the flies. We met him on the path about ten minutes later. We presented him with the shovel. He turned around with us, rather than going back to his village to check on his wife, and walked back to the village of the man who had died. We parted there. He stayed at the village where the death had occurred, and we walked on to the village of Analagak, the village of Hella, our translator.

18

MISSIONARIES: THE GOOD, THE BAD, AND THE UGLY

In 1954, a small plane flew over the Baliem Valley. There was only one passenger that day and his mission was to do something that no one else had ever done. He sat strapped into a parachute waiting until the cargo bay opened. He got up, stood on the edge of the aircraft, gazed at the Baliem Valley below him and jumped.

The man was Lloyd Van Stone. He was a missionary. With one quick leap into thin air, Christianity had arrived in the Baliem Valley.

We never did encounter any missionaries during the time we spent in the Baliem Valley. We never saw them in the small town of Wamena, nor in any of the villages we visited, but we did witness the impact they had on the Dani people.

The Dani had always been animists. They believed in the existence of demons and spirits. They believed that all life was produced by a spiritual force that was separate from matter. They believed that everything in nature has a soul independent of their physical being.

Steeped in such a long history of beliefs, you would think that the Dani would be resistant to religious change. That was not the case.

Van Stone was not killed by Dani headhunters, but rather, embraced by the Dani tribes.

Over time, other missionaries arrived in the valley. The Dani tribes took to Christianity rather quickly and we would see children in villages, naked from the waist up, with a silver cross around their neck.

The Dani did not accept all of the tenants of Christianity. They were, after all, first and foremost, a warring people. Wars and battles were fought, land was taken and lost, and combatants were wounded or killed.

The missionaries did have some positive influences on the Dani people, however. They introduced some contact with the modern world, far outside the confines of the Baliem Valley. Missionaries learned the Dani dialect, taught some of the Dani tribesmen Bahasa Indonesian so communication could occur between the Dani and the Indonesian officials who were set on exploring the valley for precious resources. Some of the Dani would be taught to read and write, and through missionary teachings the Dani would become at least somewhat aware of the outside world.

The missionaries were not able to stop polygamy which was deeply ingrained in the Dani culture. They weren't able to stop the trading of pigs for wives, nor were they able to stop the finger cutting by women.

Not all of what the missionaries did for the Dani tribes was good. They distributed clothes for the Dani to wear. When the Dani came into Wamena to trade at the local market they were instructed to wear clothing, not just the kotekas that the men wore and the orchid fiber skirts the women wore. Some did wear clothes when visiting Wamena, most did not.

The Dani did not understand the western concept of personal hygiene. They took the clothes given by the missionaries and wore them, but they never took them off. The clothes soon began to smell due to the pig's grease the Dani liberally spread over their bodies. They had never been told the importance of washing clothes. Skin rashes quickly developed, impetigo was common, and the fleas in the women's longhouses just had another place to hide.

We were only in the valley for a short period of time, but we were able to form opinions based on what we saw. The gravest error the missionaries made seemed to be they were trying to pull the Dani tribes from the Stone Age where things remained little changed for 50,000 years, into the modern age in the blink of an eye. The Dani were not psychologically prepared for this. They wanted very much to retain their culture, their way of life, but they were being dragged at breakneck speed into a world they could not fully comprehend.

Like I said, we never met any missionaries in the time we were in the valley. If we had, I think what we would have liked to have said to them is this, "Slow down. You are overloading their ability to adapt. Change is coming too quickly. Allow them to keep as much of their heritage as they can."

We never saw a Dani that we thought was having any type of mental issues. We wondered if the rapid change that was being forced upon them would change that.

What would happen if valuable mineral deposits were found in the valley? More planes would come. Those planes would carry trucks, earth moving equipment, and men. Some of those men would have guns. The Dani had already been exposed to guns. There was a small police force in Wamena. The Dani were bright people. They knew their three foot long bows and crude bamboo arrows would have no chance against such an onslaught of fire power.

If mineral deposits were found near a village, we knew what would happen to that village. Had missionaries ever tried to explain that to the Dani people, or were they simply interested in saving souls?

By the time we arrived in the Baliem Valley, missionaries had made significant inroads in converting the Dani people from animist beliefs to Christian beliefs.

We really didn't have contact with missionaries in the time we were in the Baliem Valley. The evidence of their influence was there as we witnessed children with crosses dangling from their necks. We certainly appreciated the work missionaries had done to teach Bahasa Indonesian to our translators. We realized more Indonesians were coming and the ability to communicate with them would be beneficial to the Dani tribe.

We were still left to wonder, "Did missionaries do more good than harm?" We didn't know the answer to that query. Perhaps only time would offer a definitive answer to that question.

If they did more good, life for the Dani tribes would be better. If missionaries did more harm, the Dani tribes would lose more of their culture by being exposed to the outside world.

Of course, we have to live with the fact that each visitor from the outside world, including us, would leave a footprint that could potentially change the long standing traditions of the Dani.

19

THE QUANDARY OF DANI MEN

Dani men have been warriors for generation after generation. Warring has always been a part of their DNA. Even as young boys they practice warfare. They use small bows and arrows and practice what their future lives will be like when they go on a raid against an enemy tribe.

Dani warriors would spend many hours preparing weapons before going to war. They would put boars' tusks through their nose, paint their bodies and sharpen their weapons.

Wars were ritualistic. Wars were necessary. The Dani believed in ghosts and ancestor worship. Wars were necessary to appease the ghosts of their ancestors, some of which had been killed in battle. If ancestors were appeased, the village would return to harmony and equilibrium. If one of their tribe were killed by an enemy, that death must, at some point, be avenged, even if it took years for that death to be accomplished.

The concept of war went back to a belief the Dani have in the inevitability of men dying. They believe in a story about a race between a bird and a snake. That race would determine whether man would live or die. Should man be like a snake and be able to shed his skin and live, or be like a bird and die? According to the myth, the bird won the race so man was condemned to die.

Since man was condemned to die, each Dani village had watch towers that were constantly manned as lookouts for enemy warriors approaching their village. Dani warriors were considered to be extremely fierce in battle. They were not cannibalistic, but they were definitely head hunters.

Dani men had few obligations other than being warriors. They produced offspring with their wives. Men were responsible for initially clearing the fields before planting. They would dig the trenches used to collect rainwater for the gardens during the dry season. Once the fields were cleared, their duties were done. The women took over the responsibilities of growing and harvesting the crops and watching over both the pigs and the children.

The Dani men were responsible for one other skill. It was the men, not the women, who were the weavers in Dani society. They would collect bark from the forest and spend hours rolling it on their thighs until it was rolled fine enough to be woven. They would weave the funeral belts that were to be used in the funeral ceremony when a tribe member died. The funeral belts were wrapped around the funeral pyre until just before the pyre was set on fire. The funeral belts were often decorated with small cowry shells.

The Dani valued cowry shells and bartered for them with travelers who lived near the sea where the shells were collected. The traders would then traverse the high mountains to get to the Baliem Valley, where the shells would be traded for trinkets from the Dani. The shells were not only used by the Dani for decorations, they would even be used as a type of currency. Feathers were also used as currency and trade items. The feathers were used as decorative items for warriors.

For generations, Dani men had been trained to be fierce warriors. They fought for land, they fought to appease the ghosts of the dead, and they fought to insult the enemy and wound or kill a few combatants. The purpose of wars was not to completely destroy the enemy. Wars were not about annihilation. Wars were about retribution.

Some fights were mere skirmishes. Small raiding parties would be sent out to see if they could sneak up on an unsuspecting enemy and possibly wound or kill that person. Other times alliances were established between tribes and all out wars would ensue between competing tribes. Arrows would be shot, insults would be hurled, men would be wounded; some would be killed.

The last large scale Dani war took place in 1966. Sixty warriors were killed. The Indonesian government sent in troops and forbid any future fighting. This brought an end to the battles that had taken place over millenniums.

It also changed the role of men.

By 1980, when we arrived in the Baliem Valley, fighting had been outlawed for fourteen years. By this time, Dani men were warriors in name only. They were left to clear the fields, count their pigs and wives, do a bit of weaving, and sit around and talk about the old days when they were judged by their bravery in war. In a sense, by the time we arrived, they were lost souls. They would sit around the fire in their honai at night, while smoking endless cigarettes. Older men would talk of battles in the past, give speeches of victories won, losses inflicted on the enemy, and speak of wounds, death, and warfare.

The Dani of 1980 very much wished they could return to being the warring tribes they had been in the past, where they could prove their bravery in battle, insult their enemy, and appease the ghosts of their dead.

Several years before we ventured into the Baliem Valley, Sjam had helped guide another group of foreigners to visit the valley. She had asked Willem to arrange a mock battle between different villages. The Dani men enthusiastically agreed, even though they had to dull their arrows so no one would get seriously injured. What Sjam or Willem didn't know is that these competing villages were sworn enemies of one another. The battle started out peacefully enough, with dulled arrows being shot into the air and insults shouted back and forth across the field of battle, but then things got out of hand. Villagers ran behind their huts, sharpened their arrows and began fighting in earnest. It took the chiefs of the two villages quite a while to finally convince the warriors they had to stop fighting.

That, in a nutshell, is the quandary of the Dani men. In their minds they are still warriors. They still relished the idea of returning to what their ancestors had done for hundreds of years. They would return to those days if they could, but the modern world, with laws and regulations, with guns and men in uniforms, would no longer allow wars to continue. The Dani men lost what had made them warriors in the first place. They had lost the right to fight in battles. In a sense, they had lost their manhood.

After working for a few weeks on clearing the fields, there

really wasn't much for men to do. The watch towers had all been taken down. There were no more lookouts posted high above the ground. Men no longer manned those watch towers, scanning the horizon for enemy encroachment.

The quandary of the Dani men was that there were no more enemies to look for.

In 1965 the documentary film *Dead Birds*, was finally completed after filming had ended in 1961. The film had taken nearly four years to complete and edit. The name of the documentary was taken from the Dani story about the race between the bird and the snake. *Dead Birds* represented the dead men of the different Dani tribes.

In a sense, the Dani men we encountered in 1980 were already, *Dead Birds*. They had lost the most important thing in their lives. They had lost the ability to be warriors, to prove their bravery on the field of battle, to live or die, to inflict wounds or death on their enemy. They had lost the right to appease the ghosts of dead relatives.

They had lost the essence of what it meant in to be a Dani man.

20

THE COMING AND LEAVING
OF A MAN CALLED MIKE

Every night we would end up in the honai of the village chief. After we were done trading and had our evening meal, we would gather our bedding supplies and retire to the chief's honai where village elders would join us for our nightly ritual of cigarettes, conversation, and questioning.

We were often tired after a day of trekking from one village to the next but each village was most welcoming, and genuinely interested in these white people who had come to visit them.

We would settle in, lying down on the grass covered floor of the honai and ask any question that popped into our head at any given moment. We asked the men why some kotekas were short while others were very long? Why were some kotekas curled on the end while others were straight? Did the long kotekas have anything to do with a man's . . . hmmmmm . . . equipment?

The Dani men would laugh at that last question and say, "No, it is just personal preference. Some men prefer a long koteka and others prefer a short one." They assured us it had nothing to do with a how well endowed a man was. In one village in the valley, men only wore long kotekas while at the other villages both long and short kotekas were worn.

On and on the questions went, night after night, until the cigarettes were gone or sleep started to overtake us.

We were with Wali and a number of elders one night, when someone, I forget who, asked if any of the Dani men remembered Michael Rockefeller when he visited the Baliem Valley in 1961. None of us expected the answer we got, or the information we were to receive about one of the most talked about disappearances in modern history. Wali was about to reveal a secret we didn't anticipate.

An animated discussion ensued, lead by Wali and several of the elders. When the translations were finally completed, we were all in a state of shock to learn that Wali and several other men were in attendance when Michael Rockefeller arrived in the Baliem Valley.

They were quick to correct us on one bit of information, however. They said that Michael Rockefeller told them to simply call him, "Mike" rather than "Michael."

Here we were with Dani men who actually knew 'THE' Michael Rockefeller—Michael Rockefeller, son of Governor Nelson Rockefeller, and later Vice-President of the United States. This was just too cool to believe because the disappearance of Michael Rockefeller was one of the greatest unsolved mysteries of the 20th Century. Here we were, in a Dani honai, listening to men talk about knowing Michael Rockefeller. We sat up straight, focused in on every word spoken, and I'm sure each of us thought how lucky we were to be privy to the stories we were about to hear.

Michael Rockefeller was the fifth child of Nelson A. and Mary Todhunter Rockefeller, one of the wealthiest families in America. Michael was born in May of 1938, and he was accompanied in birth by a twin sister, Mary.

To say the Rockefellers were privileged would be an understatement of gigantic proportion. The Rockefeller's had the best houses, the best cars, and the best education money could buy. Michael graduated high school from the prestigious Phillips Exeter Academy in New Hampshire where he was known as an excellent wrestler. After graduating high school, he matriculated to Harvard where he graduated cum laude with a B.A. in history and economics.

In 1960, after graduation, he served six months in the U.S. Army as a private. He was described as humble, not one to put on airs, even though he came from uncommon wealth.

Somewhere in these formative years of privileged education he became interested in art. As time passed he started to take a particular interest in primitive art. After finishing his stint in the army he accepted an invitation from the Peabody Museum of Archaeology and Ethnology to travel to the Highlands of Western Netherlands New Guinea to study the Dani tribesmen of that region.

He said he wanted to go to this remote part of the world because, "It is the desire to do something adventurous at a time when frontiers, in the real sense of the word, are disappearing."

Along on the Peabody Expedition would be Robert Gardner, a friend and film producer. Gardner would film and produce the documentary film, *Dead Birds* about the Dani culture. Rockefeller would end up being the recorder for the film. *Dead Birds* was filmed in 1961. Production of the documentary was finished in 1963 with the first viewing sometime in 1965.

Even though it was to be a documentary on the life of the Dani people there was a bit of Hollywood thrown into the production. The war scenes that were part of the documentary were not from one battle, but from several different battles between different villages. In those fight scenes there were no actors used, Dani tribesmen did get hit with arrows; injuries were inflicted. In the final production, completed in the States, the fight scenes of different battles were spliced together to make the final film.

After spending time with the Dani, Rockefeller decided to go on another trip to visit the Asmat region of Western New Guinea. His interest in primitive art is what drew him to the Asmat region. The Asmat were tribes quite different from the Highland Dani.

Rockefeller describes the Baliem Valley as a "magnificent vastness," and the Dani people as "emotionally expressive." The Asmat, on the other hand, were almost perpetually at war. He described the Asmat region as ". . . more remote country than what I have ever seen."

The Asmat were headhunters and cannibals. Perhaps Rockefeller may never have gone to the Asmat region except, the Asmat were also carvers. They carved shields, paddles, canoes, drums and ancestor poles, called Bisj Poles that would reach twenty feet into the air. It was these carvings that Rockefeller considered to be fine examples of primitive art. Rockefeller did want to study the culture of the Asmat people, but it was the carved art that Rockefeller was after.

He had been told that the finest Asmat carvings had already been traded for by earlier traders. Rockefeller, however, had a stash of trade items the Asmat had never seen before and would soon fall in love with. He had brought with him steel knives, metal axes, tobacco, and fish hooks and fish line.

Rockefeller was able to trade these simple items for the exquisite primitive art for which he'd been searching. The ancestor poles were composed of carvings of men stacked one upon the other, crocodiles, praying mantises, and symbols of headhunting.

He was able to send these wood carvings, which he was convinced weren't just primitive art, but works of exquisite art, back to America where it would later be displayed in the Metropolitan Museum of Art. Rockefeller would make other trips into the Asmat region and barter for more primitive carvings. He had no trouble bartering for the art he wanted because the Asmat had become addicted to the fish hooks, line, knives, and metal axes that they had no way of making for themselves.

The Asmat believed that any death attributed to an enemy, even to a woman or a child, must be avenged to appease the village ghosts. This avenging of death might take years to be accomplished, but it was necessary for the village to return to balance, a sense of equilibrium. In that regard they were like the Dani tribes, but in other ways they were much different people, with much different beliefs than the Dani. The Dani were content to hurl insults at their enemies with the hope of injuring a few adversaries. Battles were not intended to annihilate a rival village, nor were the Dani tribes cannibalistic.

In Asmat society, human heads were necessary for initiation rituals. Heads were used during ceremonies when young men were initiated into adulthood. Heads were decorated with feathers, shells, and stones, and placed between the young men's legs. After three days the spirit and power of the slain man would be transferred to each young man, giving him super human powers.

After a man was slain, he would be quartered and eaten by the Asmat. The head would be opened and the brains would be eaten by the warriors. Afterwards the heads would be stored, decorated, and used in life rituals. Two key parts to Asmat society included this cannibalism and the preferred annihilation of whole villages.

After victorious raids the Asmat men would sometimes drink each other's urine, have sex with other men, and even exchange wives for sexual orgies. There were reports of the Asmat men performing oral sex on the village chief after a successful raid.

After leaving the Asmat region, Rockefeller returned to the Western Highlands and continued to study the culture of the Dani people. He eventually returned to the States for a brief stay, but his desire to return to New Guinea soon brought him back, this time to study the Asmat culture.

He stayed for a while with the Dani tribes before setting off to study and trade with the Asmats. He bought a used catamaran in the coastal city of Agats. He and anthropologist Renee Wassing, along with two teen Asmat guides spent three weeks visiting 13 Asmat villages. He collected drums, carved bowls, wood carvings and bamboo horns.

Catholic priests warned Rockefeller and Wassing that the catamaran would be swamped by high waves if they ventured out onto the ocean. The catamaran was really only two long canoes lashed together with a small thatched roof hut to keep the sun off their heads.

Rockefeller and Wassing did not heed the good advice given by the priests and set off between the villages of Agats and Atsj with two teen Asmat guides on November 18, 1961. They were traversing the mouth of the Betsj River when their boat became swamped by high waves. The catamaran became flooded and soon capsized on the Arafura Sea about three miles from shore. The two Asmat teens jumped in the water and swam for shore promising to bring help. The two Asmat teens struggled through swamps and mud and did not arrive for help until after midnight.

Rockefeller and Wassing clung to the catamaran through most of the day of November 19 until Rockefeller became convinced the two teen guides had not reached safety. They were now about twelve miles from the shoreline, which was barely visible in the distance. Rockefeller decided to swim for shore. He attached two empty gas cans together, jumped into the Arafura Sea and started paddling for the distant shore. His last words were, "I think I can make it."

Michael Rockefeller was never seen again.

A rescue plane found the overturned catamaran late on November 19. The plane dropped a rubber raft to which Wassing could swim. Although Wassing was a good swimmer, he was afraid of being eaten by a shark or a salt water croc. He was rescued on the morning of November 20.

If it would have been any man other than Michael Rockefeller, the story might have gotten a one line mention in some newspapers around the world. This, of course, was no ordinary man. This was Michael Rockefeller. The New York papers carried headlines nearly every day about the search for Michael Rockefeller. The story, in fact, made headlines around the world.

The Dutch government headed an exhaustive search for Michael Rockefeller, but no trace of his body was found. Nelson Rockefeller and Michael's twin sister, Mary, paid $58,000 to rent a plane to fly into New Guinea to oversee the search party. After several weeks, the search for Michael Rockefeller's body was brought to an end.

Without a body, the official cause of death was recorded as

drowning. Michael Rockefeller may have died of exposure, a shark attack, or he may have been eaten by salt water crocodiles.

Michael Rockefeller's death remains one of the great mysteries of the 20th Century. Books have been written about it, articles have been published concerning it, a movie was made and a television show hypothesized how his death happened.

There were early rumors that Michael Rockefeller made it to shore but was killed and cannibalized by Asmat warriors. Those rumors soon subsided and the Rockefeller family publicly disavowed those theories. Their official family response was, and always has been, that Michael Rockefeller drowned at sea.

Time passed, but the rumors of what happened to Michael Rockefeller after he jumped into the Arafura Sea remain to this day. There were two incoming tides on the night of the 19th which would have aided Rockefeller, considered to be a very good swimmer, in his attempt to reach shore approximately twelve miles away. The two flotation gas cans would have kept him afloat; the water temperature was 85 degrees, so hypothermia was not a factor.

If he could swim a half mile per hour, he could have made the swim in twenty hours or less. There were two incoming tides that night pushing him to shore when he would have been most tired. Some estimates, based on sea charts, calculated he might have been a few miles closer to shore than the original guess of 12 miles.

The rumors of Michael Rockefeller making it to shore continued to build over the years. One story that took on a life of its own seems very farfetched. In this story not only did Michael Rockefeller make it to shore, but once there, he went native, joining the Asmat to live out his life in the jungle. A grainy photo was published with a number of Asmat surrounding what appears to be a white man. We had seen an albino Dani in Wamena, so it is possible that the man in the photo could have been an albino Asmat. The photo was of such poor quality that most gave little credence to the man in the photo being Michael Rockefeller.

In the documentary film, "Keep the River on Your Right," Tobias Schneebaum, who had spent considerable time with the Asmat tribes, said he spoke with Asmat cannibals who claimed they had seen something swimming in the shallow waters near the village of Otsjaned. They thought it was a crocodile or a turtle, so they went to investigate. What they found was a weary Michael Rockefeller in the shallow waters near the coast. After a heated discussion, they decided to kill Rockefeller in retaliation for the Dutch killing four prominent village leaders in 1958. They stabbed Rockefeller with a spear, carried him to a secret location and ate him.

Schneebaum's account coincided with a location where Rockefeller may well have swum to, based on the tide charts of that region.

In 2014, Karl Hoffman's book, *Savage Harvest: A Tale of Cannibals, Colonization and the Quest of Primitive Art* was published. Hoffman makes a somewhat more compelling argument that Rockefeller made it to shore, was killed by 50 Asmat warriors and eaten. What followed, according to Hoffman, was a massive cover-up by both the Dutch government and the Catholic Church.

Hoffman contends that the disappearance of Michael Rockefeller could not have come at a worse time for the Dutch government. The Dutch were trying to retain their governmental control of New Guinea while the United Nations was deciding whether Dutch New Guinea could become an independent country. If it could be proven that Michael

Rockefeller was indeed killed and eaten by cannibals, it would put the Dutch government in a bad light.

Hoffman's account differs little from Schneebaum's in that he agrees that Rockefeller swam near shore, close to the village of Otsjaned. Fifty Asmat warriors, who had been travelling by canoe at night, saw something in the water shortly after sunrise, discovered Rockefeller, recognized him because he had traded there before, debated what to do, decided to kill him and cover their bodies with his blood. They later ate him as well as his brains. They tried to keep this secret because they knew he was a powerful man.

At this point, Hoffman takes a different tack and presents a story of government and Vatican cover-up. Within two weeks, Hoffman contends, Catholic priests were informed by the Asmat that they had killed Rockefeller in retaliation for four village leaders being killed by the Dutch in 1958.

The Dutch government wanted all of this to go away, as did the Catholic Church. They did not want to lose their religious influence over the Asmat people. The missionaries were trying to convince the Asmat to no longer take part in ritual warfare and cannibalism.

Hoffman sites hundreds of letters and cables between the Dutch government and the Catholic Church who had priests along the Asmat coast. The church, according to Hoffman, did not want to lose their base of influence in the area.

The priests, Hoffman said, had names of who had Rockefeller's head, and who had other parts of his body, but they were unwilling to give this information to the Rockefeller family. After several weeks of searching for Michael's body, Nelson Rockefeller and Michael's twin sister, Mary, returned to the states. Michael Rockefeller was officially declared dead by drowning.

There were skeptics of Hoffman's claims just as there had

been skeptics of all other stories about what eventually happened to Michael Rockefeller.

If this wasn't enough suspense about what had happened to Michael Rockefeller, there is still one other story that concerned the Rockefeller family. In Paul Toohey's book, *Rocky Goes West*, the author makes a claim that Mrs. Rockefeller hired a private investigator from Australia to fly to Papua New Guinea to help uncover clues to Michael Rockefeller's disappearance. If he could provide evidence of what had happened to Michael Rockefeller, according to Toohey, a $250,000 reward would be given to the private investigator.

The investigator made contact with several Asmat who claimed to have three heads from the only whites they had ever killed. Convinced that one of these heads belonged to Michael Rockefeller, the investigator traded a boat engine for the three skulls. The investigator allegedly brought all three skulls back to the United States.

Like all other claims surrounding Michael Rockefeller's disappearance, this claim too came under scrutiny. The History Channel show "Vanishing," claims to have uncovered evidence that Mrs. Rockefeller paid a $250,000 reward to the investigator.

Whether any of these claims about Michael Rockefeller's death are true, partially true, or are downright lies, perhaps only time will tell.

We were sitting in a Dani honai with men who actually knew "Mike" as they called him and that was enough for us. We had already seen and heard so many remarkable things since we had arrived in the valley. But, this story of Michael Rockefeller, told by Dani men who had known him, simply cemented the idea that this was the greatest trip we had ever been a part of.

Where could we possibly travel after this that could compare to our journey into the Baliem Valley? We would always remember the stories we had heard, what we had seen, the natural beauty of the valley, and most of all the generosity and kindness and its people.

21

A LAST DANCE WITH THE DANI TRIBE

We walked at least seven miles each day and certainly there were several days when the walk was at least ten miles or more. The pace was never fast or hurried, however. Time was irrelevant to the Dani tribe and we took our cue from them. If we met other Dani tribe members on our walks, everyone stopped walking and a conversation would ensue after the obligatory laoak and narok greetings. The conversation would last as long as someone had something to say. After a few days, it didn't seem all that strange to us when we saw these muscular men embrace each other in this gentle fashion. Even the laoak and narok were conveyed in a voice barely above a whisper.

The Dani embrace was from forearm to forearm with the hands resting at the other fellow's elbows. There was this dichotomy about the Dani. When dressed in boar's tusks, bone breast plates and dried pigs testicles around their elbows, the Dani men took on the appearance of the fiercest warriors you might ever encounter. They were indeed frightening in their appearance once they were dressed in their "going to war" outfits, and it was not at all hard to imagine what they must have been like during a raiding party. Yet in their inner dealings with other villagers they were gentle, kind, and considerate with their time.

Their children, from what we observed, mimicked their parents. I never saw a Dani child chastised for their behavior or disciplined in any manner. They played in mud puddles and were carried in the women's nokens when they were small. As they grew older, they helped care for the pigs which were let out during the day and collected and put inside the wooden village walls at night.

We had gotten used to the ebb and flow of village life in just a few short days. Each Dani knew their task and did it without complaint. Yes, the women worked harder than the men, but they seemed to accept their role in life and did not seem unhappy with the fate of being born female. They worked in their gardens from early morning until late afternoon, digging, hoeing, cultivating, and watering the plants that sustained them. They would come out of their fields as the sun was waning, muddy from the knees down, their nokens laden with greens and sweet potatoes. They would walk back to their village, enter the long house of the women, and be ready to prepare the evening meal when someone declared they were hungry. There were no set meal times and they allowed hunger pangs to dictate when it was time to eat.

One night, towards the end of our stay with the Dani tribe, our guide told us there would be a village dance that evening. Our expectations were high, sensing that the Dani surely had an elaborate form of dancing that they were about to demonstrate for us. In that regard, we were soon to be very disappointed. The Dani way of dancing had to be one of the simplest dance steps anyone had ever invented. Most of the women stayed in the longhouse and began a chant. The Dani men, picking up on the chants, would do a sort of shuffling trot from one side of the village to the other. Once the men reached the end of the courtyard, the women would repeat the chant and the men would shuffle back in the direction they had come from.

That was it. That was the entire dance. Simplicity personified in a slow, shuffling trot.

It didn't take our group of six long to decide that the Dani dance was much too rudimentary. We were all up for a dance, something we had not yet done in any of the villages we had visited, but this shuffling motion just wasn't going to cut it. We were all teachers, and it didn't take long before our teaching instincts took over.

Once again Gene Wasosky led the way. He stuffed a koteka down the front of his trousers, put a feather plume in the end of it, put a chest plate made from pig bones around his neck and he put on a crazy little hat that he had brought along on the trip. Instead of just shuffling back and forth, Gene would take a few steps and raise his arms into the air and give a shout. The rest of our small party quickly joined in and the cadence, tempo, and rhythm of the dance quickly accelerated.

The Dani tribesmen caught on immediately. They loved this newer, upbeat tempo. Soon they were mimicking us, their smiles small sunbeams lighting up the evening sky. After a few minutes we added a small jump to our raised arm motion and like obedient students, the Dani followed suit.

The Dani had been teaching us so much each day, it felt good to be able to return the favor.

We had a terrific time at the dance. We danced, we laughed, and we made fun of Gene with the koteka sticking out of his trousers. It was our first opportunity to let our hair down, unwind, and let our exuberance show.

The Dani seemed to possess an endless endurance. As much as we enjoyed the dance, fatigue began to set in after an hour or so. The Dani didn't seem to notice. They were too caught up in the new dance moves to pay much attention to our lagging foot falls.

A fire was lit in the courtyard and our shadows were cast on the honai walls. A few of our band of six danced on for a while longer but sleep beckoned us. We took our sleeping gear to the Chief's honai where we talked for some time, listened to the chants of the women and the jumping and shouting of the men until sleep took us prisoners.

It wasn't until the next day that we were told the dance was actually a competition between the Dani men and the women. The Dani women chanted and the Dani men would dance. The competition was to see whether the men or women would give up first. The women, we learned, gave their final chant at 5:30 a.m. The men did not respond. The last of the men had departed to their honai at last succumbing to sleep. The women won the contest. It may have been the one and only time the Dani women ever defeated the Dani men at anything.

I hope the women took pride in that victory.

As I danced away the night, a revelation slowly came over me. I realized that this dance with the Dani tribe would be both my alpha and my omega. The thought morphed until it finally crystallized and it became abundantly clear that I would never dance with the Dani tribe again, just as surely as I realized I would never again return to the Baliem Valley.

I had witnessed many amazing things in this journey. I had seen the 400 year old mummy of Aikima, watched salt be gathered in a brine pool in the mountains, met men who told me stories of Michael Rockefeller, saw young girls with a portion of a finger freshly severed in the name of love for a deceased relative, and I had witnessed both the gentleness and the bravery of a tribe of people who were still living much as they had for generations.

I also realized that life is not static. Just as the Dani wanted to retain their culture, they also encouraged us to tell others of their valley and encourage them to come to the Baliem to visit and trade. The Dani were intelligent people, but they knew little of the outside world. The thought of retaining their culture was a fantasy. I had come to like them too much to tell them this, although perhaps I should have at least tried. More people would indeed come to their valley, and with them would come monumental change. Not all of this change would be good.

We, in fact, had already helped perpetuate that change. As we were leaving the Baliem Valley, we gave away some shoes, socks, shorts and shirts. The Dani tribesmen wanted them and we had no further use for these items so it was an easy parting gift. It would lighten our load but it would burden them. It would create a want they had never had before.

I had given away a 7-Up can with a pop top tab that became an earring.

We had visited the Dani tribes and changed their culture ever so slightly in our short stay with them. That was on us, and it was not something of which to be terribly proud.

I made a promise to myself that night as I danced. I promised myself that I would never return to the Baliem Valley, because I knew that if I ever returned I would see things I did not want to see; change I did not want to happen. I wanted to remember the valley just as I had first seen it, the chiefs, Wali and Killian, women working in the fields, the beauty of a morning sunrise as the sun peaks over the mountain tops, the innocent smiles of the villagers, the gentleness and kindness of the people.

The trip was almost over.

I would not return.

I wanted this last dance with the Dani tribe to be my lasting memory.

22

SAYING GOODBYE

We stayed one night in Obaharok's village even though Obaharok wasn't there. We had our usual fitful night of sleep battling mosquitoes and the dirty, run down feel of the village didn't improve our mood. Whenever we were outside, the honai flies were everywhere. Fighting the battle with the flies was a losing proposition. You would swat them away, but they would simply circle and land once again.

We awoke early the next morning to our usual fare for breakfast of tea, toast, and rice. I think we all consumed less food each day due to the lack of variety in our diet. The Dani, of course, had it worse than us with the inevitable meal of sweet potatoes and a variety of greens from their gardens. At least we had a choice between tea, tea mixed with Tang, and the remnants of snacks we had packed for the trip.

The snacks we shared with any Dani men close to us during breaks we took while walking. I never saw a Dani who turned down a snack. I imagine they liked to try any food that was different from their mundane menu. They were more than happy to try any of our food, but I never heard them comment if they liked it or not. They simply ate what we offered. I think it was just their way of finding out a little of our culture. They always seemed keen to learn as much about us as they could. Food always seems to bridge any cultural gap and it was no different in the Baliem Valley.

After breakfast we left Obaharok's village. This turned out to be the one village we were more than happy to leave because of how dirty it was, plus we would be leaving behind the swarms of flies that were driving us to distraction.

We walked for a few hours before arriving at Analagak Village, home of Hella, one of our interpreters. This gave us one last time to trade. By this time, I was loaded down with all the things I wanted to buy. I wasn't sure what I was going to do with the items I had bought once I got everything back to Jakarta, so I told myself I was all purchased out. Gene Wasosky more than balanced out my lack of purchases. He had a real fondness for primitive art and had a huge collection from previous purchases he had made in Jakarta. He continued to make trades while I was content to watch negotiations unfold.

The villagers did not recognize the green 500 Rupiah notes we had brought in with us. In hindsight, we would have been better off simply bringing in the red 100 Rupiah notes that they were becoming somewhat familiar with. Hella had to convince his own village that one 500 Rupiah note was worth five red 100 Rupiah notes. I don't think it really made a difference as the Dani were always willing to barter. I don't think they really had a sense of what something was worth nor did it make any particular difference to them.

They could always make more arrows, spears, and bows. To make items they had made all their lives cost them nothing but their time, and in the Baliem Valley time was not a rare commodity. Men might spend hours rolling bark across their thighs until it was thin enough for weaving. Whatever time it took, was simply the time needed to complete the task at hand.

We stayed at Analagak Village until we had eaten lunch and then started our last trek towards Wamena. After we had walked for an hour we climbed up the side of a mountain and had one last magnificent view of the Baliem Valley before us. We descended, then back over another hill, and finally down one last time to the basin below.

Ahead lay our final destination of Wamena, where, if the plane arrived the next day, we would fly out of the Baliem Valley and back to Jayapura.

Before we got back to Wamena, we first had to cross a river via a narrow wooden, swinging bridge. As we approached the river, we noticed a difference in the Dani tribesmen who had accompanied us. They seemed more furtive and apprehensive, looking around frequently, obviously anxious about something. I asked Willem what was up with the change in attitude. Willem said that this was enemy territory from past wars. Even Killian had only been in this part of the valley once before. Warring between tribes had already been outlawed for nearly a decade and a half, but the Dani had long memories. This land was not land they were familiar with. It was land of their sworn enemies and that knowledge made them nervous. Old ways die hard and it was a part of the Dani DNA to still be looking out for an ambush.

We reached a river of brown water and indeterminate depth. There were currents that swirled and carried debris downstream. The bridge was about 150 meters long. It was a suspension bridge with metal cables stretching across the river. The platform of the bridge was a series of uneven wooden planks held together by vines connected to the steel cables. The wooden planks were just wide enough to accommodate one person at a time. There were gaps between the planks. They were not wide gaps, just wide enough that you became aware of each step you took; making sure your foot was firmly planted on the next plank before proceeding.

The steel cables were high on both ends of the bridge, but they swooped down low near the mid-point of the crossing. When you got to the middle of the bridge, it required you to crouch down and cling to the cables which were now below waist level. To make the crossing even more interesting, the bridge swayed from side to side as you traversed the 450 feet to the other side. I wouldn't say it was a dangerous crossing, but it did elevate your pulse rate.

Just as we were about to make the crossing a very strange thing happened. Yacoom, the tribe comedian who was always making someone laugh, and Killian, a chief who seemed to fear nothing, both refused to cross the bridge. Both men had been to the bridge once before and they had both chosen to swim across the river rather than take their chances with the swinging bridge. If Willem had not stepped in to stop them, they would have chosen this option again. Willem told them they could not swim the river under any circumstances because he did not trust the swirling currents. They could wait to cross after some of the tribesmen demonstrated the safety of crossing via the bridge.

When Yacoom started across the bridge, it was time for his friends to finally get a laugh at his expense. Yacoom got about a third of the way across the bridge when his friends, not far behind him on the bridge, started jumping up and down. The bridge swayed from side to side, Yacoom crouched lower and held on to the cables for dear life, and his friends hooted and hollered before finally letting Yacoom cross to the other side. His friends had a great time seeing the discomfort Yacoom was experiencing making the crossing.

I noticed that when Killian crossed there was no jumping on the bridge. No one was going to make fun of the chief, and Killian crossed without incident.

The crossing took quite a while, perhaps as much as an hour. The six of us took our time, stopping in the middle of the bridge, squatting down before turning around to get our picture taken. It was a windy day and the wooden bridge swayed a lot, especially near the middle where the cables came down to just a couple of feet from the wood planks. It was an interesting crossing in that it was the first and only time we saw the Dani tribesmen show apprehension about anything.

The last 45 minute walk to Wamena was at a very brisk pace. The Dani men broke into a chanting song as we marched across the landing strip of the airport and back into town.

I was really looking forward to a shower, or a bath, not having been able to bathe since we landed in the valley. We stayed in a room that had a bathtub, but when I turned on the spigot only a muddy sludge came out. A hot bath would have to wait at least one more day.

A room with a real bed never looked so good. After a dinner of rice, we all got our first good night's sleep.

Some of the porters left to go back across the hanging bridge at night. They would stay in the last village we passed and then continue on home in the morning.

Killian, his wife, whose name I never learned, and Yacoom stayed near the market place with friends.

The next morning while we were eating our breakfast of rice and toast, Killian, Yacoom, and Hella were collecting our bags. All the things we had traded for were wrapped in cardboard for the flight to Jayapura.

Pam had woken up in a rash. We thought it was either lice bites or some type of bed bug. Gene and Kathy Wasosky soon came down with the same affliction.

We kept looking at the sky, wondering if the plane would arrive, when at the appointed time we saw the plane descend over the mountains. It seemed to hang in the sky, hovering like some gigantic praying mantis, and then it dropped to the tarmac in a rush and came to rest just a few feet from us.

After several last photos, it was time to say narok and laoak and board the plane.

The last time I saw Killian he was still standing by the small terminal building as the plane taxied down the runway. Willem said he saw him as we lifted off, still standing, starring at the plane.

I couldn't help wondering what was going through his head. Surely he must have been thinking of a time several months in the future when he and Wali would board the plane to fly to Jayapura and see the big boats and sleep in a bed.

Our other life called; there was no way any of us could stick around another two months to take a plane ride with Killian and Wali. Even with that acknowledgement there was still a sense of loss that we wouldn't see Killian and Wali board a plane, see their expressions as the plane taxied down the runway and lifted off, unencumbered by earthly bounds, flying off into the unknown.

I hoped it would be a clear day and they would pass over the neatly groomed gardens, see women hoeing with their sticks and irrigation trenches filled with water. I hope they got a clear view of the valley they had lived in, but had been prisoners of all their lives. They would be able to at last view their valley from a new vantage point as they climbed up and over higher mountains, leaving Wamena behind, heading towards a world they had only dreamed about.

If I could have stayed, I would have been willing to pay a lot of money to have been on that maiden flight with Killian and Wali. Some dreams die hard. I knew I would not be on that flight, but still, I dreamed.

I was left with one question that would go unanswered. I wondered if their visit to modern life would be as amazing to them as our visit to the Baliem Valley had been to us.

23

RETURN TO JAYAPURA

The return to Jayapura was uneventful. We had clear skies and no turbulence. The jungle was still green and impenetrable; the rivers still a muddy brown. None of those views had changed in the time we were gone. What had changed, in the short time we were in the Baliem Valley, was us. We had witnessed something few people would ever have the opportunity to experience. We had the privilege of visiting a world that had changed little in thousands of years. The Dani people were primitive, but they could not have treated us with more kindness. They were patient, understanding, accommodating, helpful and sharing. They showed us the many layers of their culture and asked questions about ours. They knew they weren't worldly, but we learned they were intelligent, thoughtful and introspective.

We came away from the experience thinking that the Dani tribe had taught us a hell of a lot more than we would ever be able to teach them.

We thought they were an absolute marvel.

We landed on the tarmac at Sentani Airport and made our way through the terminal, collected our bags and all of the items we had traded for with the different Dani villages.

I weighed myself on the baggage scales as I was waiting for our bags to arrive. I had weighed 184 pounds when I boarded the plane that would take me and my friends to Wamena. The scale now registered 172 pounds. I bought a coke and downed it quickly. Before the day was done, I had drunk nine more cokes. I hadn't realized how dehydrated I had become in the time we were gone. We all got very tired of tea, or tea with Tang mixed in so apparently I just stopped drinking liquids.

We took the 45 minute ride from Sentani Airport back into town. We stopped in a museum on the way and spent an hour looking around. I can't even remember what we saw. All I know is that it could not compare to where we had been and what we had seen.

It is amazing how just a short time can change your perspective. I had viewed Jayapura as a dirty, congested, and oil coated harbor town. There hadn't been anything that interested me when we had first arrived in Jayapura just a short time ago.

We walked around town as the sun was going down. We saw a tanker unloading its cargo of flour at the docks. The tanker was enormous. There were cranes picking up huge loads of sacked flour in one swift motion. They were mechanical monsters, gulping thousands of pounds of flour at a time. There were trucks with over-sized tires that would transport the flour to huge warehouses where the flour would be stacked once again. Eventually the flour would be moved again where it would be used to bake some product for which the Dani tribes had no use.

We got to our hotel, got checked in by a smiling girl in a nice outfit, given our room keys and had our bags carried to our room by a hotel worker.

We took our first bath since we had left for the Baliem Valley. I had my first change of clean clothes in days. After we got cleaned up, we all went out to a restaurant. There was an extensive menu to look over before we made our selections, and thankfully sweet potatoes did not appear on the menu.

Later we went to bed, a real bed, with a mattress and no lice. We slept the sleep of the dead.

We got up the next day with the knowledge we would have one more day in Jayapura. We were to be given a free day since we had lost the first day of the trip, the return flight was not until the next day. Willem decided to lead us on a day trip to an island off the coast of Jayapura. On the way to the island we stopped at a village built on stilts. Once again we were surrounded by villagers who owned pigs. The pigs stayed in the houses which were perched over the water. The houses were mere shacks made of rattan siding and tin roofs.

When the tide went out, the pigs were released down a ramp where they used their snouts to dig for food. When the tides began to come in, a ramp was lowered and the pigs trotted back up to the houses.

We spent an hour or so at the village and then boarded the boat for the short trip to the island. We had all spent plenty of time on islands, but this particular island was fantastic. We had the whole island to ourselves. The ocean was the temperature of bath water. It felt great to soak in the azure waters and let the aches and pains of our trip slowly slip away. There were no currents and we could walk out a long way in the water before we were up to mid-torso. We were six weary travelers soaking up vitamin D, rejuvenating, allowing the sea to caress us as small waves lapped against our weary bodies, making us whole again.

There was one teenage boy on the island picking coconuts. He brought some of those coconuts to us, we quickly struck a bargain, and we bought the coconuts he had for a very small amount of money. The teen went away happy and we never saw him again the rest of the day. A picnic lunch had been packed for us so we whiled away the day soaking the soreness out of joints, eating fresh coconuts as well as food we had not set eyes on in days. The weather was great, the water soothing. No doubt we enjoyed the day more because of where we had been, sleeping on bare ground, swatting mosquitoes, eating the same meal day after day. We were once more in our element. We had a splendid day.

We walked along the beach, thinking that someday a rich businessman would invest money and turn the island into a beach paradise, when we came across something of a bygone era. A few feet off the beach in shallow water, partially sunken in the sand, waves gently slapping against its hulk, was a World War II Allied landing craft. It brought us back to the reality of war. Modern warfare had come to New Guinea, men from a number of countries had been killed, and many of those remained where they fell, in the jungles of New Guinea.

There were caves everywhere. Whether you believe the atomic bomb should or should not have been dropped on Japan, is up to you. The jungle, the foliage, and the caves would have dragged the war out for months, if the most destructive weapon ever invented by man had not been used.

We returned to town with sun burns and smiles. We would spend one more night in Jayapura before heading off on the next phase of our vacation.

The next day all of us were on a plane heading east to Sulawasi to visit the area called Tanah Toraja. We were especially interested in witnessing the rituals used at the end of life. They are famous for the elaborate ceremonies to celebrate the life of any deceased relative. It ended up being another great adventure, but that is a story for another time.

24

AFTERTHOUGHTS

Nearly forty years have passed since we ventured into the Baliem Valley of Irian Jaya. In those intervening years, I have had the opportunity to travel to many countries in Europe and Asia. New Zealand is a beautiful country; the fjords of Norway are breathtaking. The beaches in Bali and Thailand are tranquil and a joy in which to swim and snorkel. Angkor Wat and the many other wats in Cambodia are architectural wonders. The lasting memories of the jangling bells of the donkey trains climbing through the mountains of Nepal are permanent reminders of another great trip. Crawling through the Cu Chi tunnels of Vietnam was an eye opening experience. There are times when I think of those countries and many others that I have had that opportunity to visit. Those thoughts are fleeting, only present in your mind for a few moments as you reminisce, before they are quickly put aside to deal with the activities of daily life.

The Dani tribes of the Baliem Valley, however, carry memories that stay with me year after year. I might hear something on the nightly news about a conflict in Irian Jaya, or see a photograph of the island of New Guinea and I am instantly transported back to the trip we took many years ago. I once again can picture the sights and sounds we experienced as we walked through a beautiful valley. I still find I think of Irian Jaya on a more frequent basis than any other trip I have been on.

I'm sure that Wali and Killian, respected chiefs of their Dani villages, are both dead now. I wonder if Killian was ever forced to take another wife so he might sire a male heir to replace him as chief of Wiyagoba Village. There may be no Dani alive who remembers Michael Rockefeller's visit to the Baliem Valley in 1961.

There are these questions, and so many more that go unanswered. Small snippets of information do occasionally slip out of the valley, over the 10,000 foot mountains peaks and meandering rivers of Irian Jaya and into the newspapers and broadcasts of the modern world.

Mineral deposits were indeed discovered in Papua. Gold and copper deposits with an estimated market value of approximately a hundred billion dollars were unearthed. The Indonesian government signed an agreement with a U. S. company, Freeport McMoran, to mine those deposits. The Freeport McMoran's Grasberg mine became a quasi-Indonesian company under Indonesian President Sukarno. It also became Indonesia's largest tax payer. The subsequent tailings from the mine have choked the rivers the Papuans depended on for their living. The fish, oysters, and shrimp the Papuans gathered from those rivers have been almost completely killed off by pollution.

Few Papuans were hired to work at the mines and Papuans now have one of the lowest income levels in Indonesia. Land has been taken from the Papuans by Freeport McMoran and other settlers.

Indonesia uses a policy of transmigration. The government moves Indonesians from overcrowded islands like Java to other lands in Indonesia so they might, "assimilate into the local culture." Often these Indonesians have no choice in regard to moving. They are simply rounded up and moved. Over one million Indonesians have been moved to West Papua. The indigenous Papuans have become a minority population in their own land. By 2020, estimates are that ethnic Papuans will make up only 29% of the population.

West Papuans still carry on their fight for Independence. An estimated 500,000 Papuans have been killed in their fight for self-rule. Indigenous tribes have been racked by poverty, disease, and oppression. Mining towns have become nesting grounds for drinking, drugs, and prostitution. The highest rates of HIV in Indonesia are in these towns.

Recently a conflict arose between Freeport McMoran and the Indonesian government. Freeport subsequently fired 30,000 workers, exacerbating an already poverty ridden region.

As one Papuan put it, "It is an island without law."

The Baliem Valley was not immune to being dragged into the 21st Century. The Dani tribes are no longer the Stone Age people we witnessed many years ago. Over sixty per cent of the Dani are now categorized as Christian, although polygamy still exists.

The government run transmigration policy brought other problems. The Baliem Valley of the past had almost no known diseases. Transmigration brought with it the first cases of venereal disease to the Dani tribes.

The Indonesian government decided that the Dani should move out of their traditional honai huts. They built cement block houses and moved many of the Dani into a type of housing they were not used to; houses that were not well suited for the Baliem Valley. The Dani did not like this new arrangement and moved back to the honai of their respective villages.

The cement block houses did not go to waste. The Dani moved their pigs into the houses.

The barter system eventually broke down as the traditional way of trading. As the Indonesian Rupiah replaced bartering, part of their culture was lost. Word reached us a few years ago that the Dani now charge visitors money for taking their photographs, something unheard of when we visited them.

There are modern hotels in Wamena today that accommodate visitors who make the easy flight to Wamena on modern aircraft outfitted with navigational equipment that allows them to fly in any kind of weather.

Indonesia started "Operasi Koteka" to get the Dani to give up their traditional dress. Air dropped clothes were supplied to the Dani people as a way of convincing them to change the way they dress. Some still cling to the old ways, living simple lives in the countryside as they have done for years. Many of the young have buckled under social pressure and now wear modern clothing.

Tourism and making money are rapidly leaving the old culture behind.

It would have been nice, if somehow, the Dani culture could have been kept in isolation from the outside world and only studied by sociologists who would not have tried to change them.

More and more the Dani are speaking the Indonesian language while allowing the Dani dialects to become relegated as an afterthought. These local dialects may soon be lost.

Are the Dani really better off today than when we saw them all those years ago? Their life expectancy is longer, and they have learned more of the outside world, but they have given up a great deal of their culture in return.

As I think about the Dani people, what we saw when we were there in 1980, and what they are today, I am reminded of the quote from Pogo: "We have met the enemy and it is us."

The Dani have only changed because we changed them.

I think often of the trip into the Baliem Valley and our visit to the Dani tribes who live there. I am so thankful to have had that opportunity to visit them when their culture and natural environment was still pretty much intact.

I made a promise on the night I had a last dance with the Dani. I promised myself I would never return to the Baliem Valley. Almost forty years have passed, but I have kept that promise. I knew it was the right decision then, just as I know it is the right decision all these years later.

I had my last dance with the Dani tribe.

It was a beautiful dance.

That is how I always want to remember it.

Left to right: Art Dunn, Harlan Flick, Joan Dunn, Kathy Wasosky, Gene Wasosky. Missing from this picture is Pam Flick, as she was the photographer.

25

EPILOGUE: WHERE ARE THEY NOW?

Six of us went into the Baliem Valley in December of 1980. Five of us are living today.

As I began writing this book, I knew I would need some input from the other members of the trip so I reached out to them to get their reflections and memories of that eventful journey.

A few years ago my wife and I spent 24 hours in Singapore. We hadn't been back to Singapore in years and this gave us a chance to reconnect with a student we had taught in China and also a chance to see Gene Wasosky. We hadn't seen Gene in over 30 years so we spent time getting caught up on our lives and talking about places we had traveled to since we had last seen each other.

We booked the cheapest room we could find at a cost of $125. The towels were thread bare and there was one well worn thin blanket on the bed. We still remember being able to book 4 and 5 star rooms for $25 a night when we first visited Singapore in the late 70s. This visit certainly brought back memories of Singapore of a bygone era and its leader Lee Kwon Yew. Premier Lee had transformed Singapore to a city-state that was the envy of the rest of the world. He died at the age of 91 on March 23, 2015. One point seven million Singaporeans paid their respects to Premier Lee, standing in the rain for six hours for a ten second viewing of the body.

All of Singapore wept.

We had dinner with the Singaporean student we had coached in China and the next day we caught up with Gene over lunch at the Singapore American Club. Gene has reinvented himself so many times over the years that it is hard to keep track of all the things he has done. Gene left Jakarta International School in 1984. He went to work for Dresser Industries as a Drilling Fluid Engineer, sometimes called a mud engineer. Gene continued to work for Dresser until 1989. In '89 Gene started his own business, Expat World and moved full time to Singapore.

Expat World is a subscription newsletter dealing with all things outside the United States whether that is travel, relocation, deals on hotels or extended cruises around the world. Gene has travelled to all seven continents and to 173 countries. He recently went to Antarctica so he could lay claim to having travelled to all seven continents.

As Singapore became more and more expensive, Gene began splitting his time between Singapore and Phuket, Thailand. He recently just moved again to Hawaii where he has a home. His plan is to split time between Hawaii and Thailand.

Gene and I talked on the phone recently and he mentioned he still has most of his primitive collection, although it has been stored in various storage facilities around the country for a number of years.

While Gene travels extensively, he never wants to get too far away from the tropics. One of his favorite lines is: "If I don't see a palm tree on the horizon, I'm not staying in that location very long."

At one point he began painting, although he had never painted anything before in his life. He had no training in art, but decided he would take a few lessons and give painting a try. He told me he took to art, "like a duck to water." He has sold some of his paintings for as much as $3,000 each.

Gene told me he considers the Dani trip to be one of the top five trips he has ever taken.

Gene and Kathy Wasosky eventually separated. I was able to track Kathy down in a small city in central Florida. She also left Jakarta International School in 1984 and accepted a job at Singapore American School and taught there for 19 years. She eventually returned to the states to help her only sister get a business off the ground in Pittsburgh. Five years ago she moved to Florida to help care for her aging parents.

When we spoke on the phone, she mentioned she hadn't travelled internationally since returning to the states and had recently let her passport lapse. She had taught in American Samoa, Istanbul, Turkey, Jakarta and Singapore. She seemed happy enough to set down roots. She still makes pottery and goes to a few craft sales each year.

Kathy mentioned several things about the trip. She

mentioned the Amulet and the kerfuffle that caused with the Dani tribesmen. She said she went to sleep that night wondering if she would wake up in the morning or if her head would be an ornament on some Dani spear.

I guess I wasn't the only one nervous about the events of that evening.

Kathy also mentioned another incident that dealt with Dani hospitality that I had forgotten about. She mentioned the day we went up the mountain to see how salt was gathered. She had hurt her knee on the way up the mountain and was limping badly on the way down. Two Dani men, seeing her discomfort, approached her and spoke just a couple of words to each other. They each got on opposite sides of Kathy, lifted her up under the arms and carried her down the mountain. Kathy said her feet did not touch ground until she was off the mountain and on level terrain. That story is just another illustration of the kindness and generosity of the Dani people.

Kathy told a story of taking a snack break while walking between villages. She went through her day pack and took out a box of Wheat Thin crackers. Bugs had gotten into the Wheat Thins so she discarded the package. Several of the Dani porters who were accompanying us gave her a very quizzical look as if to say, "Lady what are you doing throwing away food?" Kathy got up to leave and the two Dani porters picked up the package of Wheat Thins, bugs included, and ate them.

Art Dunn was the only one of the six that proved a challenge contacting. Through mutual friends we knew he lived in Florida, but whenever I would place a call it would go to voice mail. After numerous unsuccessful attempts, I got a different number and we finally were able to talk on the phone and get caught up after almost 40 years.

Art and Joan left JIS in 1986. They returned to Michigan where Art took a job at Ferris State. He was put in charge of international student recruitment. Eventually he became an Adjunct Professor and taught several classes. They lived in a cabin on a river and ended up staying at Ferris State for two years.

They decided to return to international education and took jobs at an international school in Caracas, Venezuela. The stayed there until it became politically unstable and returned to the states where they both accepted jobs at Pfeiffer University in Charlotte, North Carolina.

They retired in 2006 and moved to Dunedin, Florida. They bought a condo and settled into retirement. Sadly, Joan developed a brain disease and passed away in 2014. Art is still adjusting to life without Joan.

Art has fond memories of the trip into the Baliem Valley and he related many of the same stories that we all remembered from the trip. The most telling memory was of the kindness and helpfulness of the Dani people. He had a balky knee and the Dani helpers went out of their way in guiding him across narrow bridges and downed trees. He also remembered the softness of the Dani voices as they embraced each other and whispered, "Wha, wha, wha," the Dani sound of endearment.

If my wife and I had not returned to JIS for a third year, we would have missed out on the Dani trip. Thankfully we decided to stay on one last year after our initial two year contract finished, giving us this once in a lifetime opportunity to travel into the Baliem Valley.

We returned for second semester of the 1980-81 school year and a strange thing happened. We signed on for one more year. Instead of staying two years, we ended up staying four. We did leave Indonesia after the '81-'82 school year and returned to Wisconsin. We missed family, sports, changing seasons, brats, cheese, ice cream, the Badgers and the Packers. We spent our first year back living in Stoughton where Pam had a job teaching at the high school. I spent the year subbing in local school districts. The next school year we were both hired at Prairie du Chien Public Schools where we would spend a total of two years.

Sometime during that first year back in America, our conversations seemed more and more to be discussions about JIS and teaching and living abroad. We both missed what we had in Jakarta, a great school system, engaged students who were highly motivated, comfortable living conditions, and the ability to travel to exciting places. What we thought we were missing in the States was still there, but there was also an itch to return to overseas life. As time passed, our conversations kept returning to the excitement of overseas life and we knew the itch we were experiencing would have to be scratched.

We went to a recruitment trip for overseas schools our second year back in America. We were offered jobs at an international school, but had reservations about how long we would be at that particular location. We turned down the job offer and started our third year back on American soil. As soon as we started our third year teaching in America, we knew we wanted to return overseas and make international education our vocation.

We contacted several overseas schools that we thought would be a good fit for us and Jakarta International School offered us teaching positions to return to Indonesia. We couldn't sign the contracts fast enough.

We returned to Jakarta in 1985 and would spend the next twelve years teaching and coaching at that fine institution as well as travelling extensively. We returned to Wisconsin in 1997 when our son was four years old so he could ride a bike, play soccer, baseball, and basketball. We wanted him to experience what it was like to be an American kid. We stayed in Wisconsin until our son finished his freshmen year in high school. We had been offered a variety of overseas jobs in those intervening years, but now the whole situation had to be evaluated to assure it fit the needs of two adults and one young teenager. The fit never seemed exactly right for all of our needs, so we stayed on American soil for 10 years.

In 2008 we were offered teaching jobs in Suzhou, China. We were mostly driven by a strong desire for our son to experience an international setting, so we packed our bags and were off to China where we taught from 2008 to 2011. Our son graduated from Suzhou Singapore International School in 2011 and we returned to Wisconsin where we live today.

We started out never wanting to leave our roots in Wisconsin and eventually became enamored with international life. We missed some things from being gone from America that long, but we gained much more in all of the various experiences of living abroad.

We're now retired and live in a small town in Wisconsin. Our overseas teaching days are over, but we travel extensively each winter. We are still Wisconsinites, but our bones feel better in the warm weather of the tropics rather than fight the cold and gloom of Wisconsin winter.

Asia, the sights, sounds, smells and yes the palm trees, calls each winter.

We answer that call, gladly.

ABOUT THE AUTHOR

Harlan Flick was born and raised in De Soto, Wisconsin. He is a graduate of the University of Wisconsin-Platteville. His life has been spent as an educator teaching in public schools in Fennimore, Waunakee, Prairie du Chien and Richland Center, Wisconsin. He then broadened his horizons with teaching stints at international schools in Jakarta, Indonesia for 16 years and Suzhou, China for 3 years.

His overseas experience has taken him to more than 25 countries and allowed many opportunities to travel. Some highlights he has had include: walking the beaches of Bali, trekking out of Kathmandu, Nepal, visiting the Taj Mahal in India, viewing Paris from atop the Eiffel Tower, viewing the ancient temples of Angkor Wat, Cambodia, walking on the Great Wall, visiting Shangri-La, and viewing the Terra Cotta warriors of Xi'an, China. He has stood next to prehistoric Stonehenge in England, boated up the Fjords of Norway, spent time with stone-age Dani tribesmen in Irian Jaya, ridden elephants in Thailand and spent a month walking the streets of the walled city of Chang Mai.

All of these experiences have helped shape his view of the world and made him appreciate the beauty that is the driftless area of southwest Wisconsin.

He lives in Richland Center, Wisconsin with his wife, son, and his many fly rods. He may be reached via email at phflick@gmail.com.